Our understanding ⟨...⟩ of how we feel and the way we act, especially when it comes to matters of sexuality and gender. This is a helpful, honest and sympathetic guide for those looking for solid ground to stand on. Highly recommended!
—**Sam Allberry**, pastor, author of *Is God Anti-Gay?* and *What God Has To Say About Our Bodies*

Andrew has written something remarkable and significant. With heartfelt honesty about his own experiences, he lays out a compassionate and clear case for a God-given identity. This is essential reading for anyone working with young people who may be struggling with sexuality or gender issues, but it will also be deeply challenging for anyone who wants to better understand their Christian identity.
—**Robin Barfield**, associate minister for children and families at Christ Church, Wharton and a visiting/adjunct lecturer at Oak Hill, Union and Cliff College

Sociologically aware, pastorally sensitive, biblically rooted – Andrew Bunt's work provides a helpful introduction to why questions of identity are crucial to mission and ministry today, especially amongst emerging generations.
—**Gareth Crispin**, lecturer in practical theology and programme lead for BA Mission and Ministry, Cliff College

Parents need this book! The topics of identity, gender and sexuality are suddenly everywhere. Andrew reassures us that God is not taken by surprise. His better story is all we need to help our children navigate today's changing cultural landscape.
—**Ed Drew**, Director, Faith in Kids

Finding Your Best Identity is a warm, thoughtful, and life-affirming approach to some very deep questions. Accessible to all, Andrew tells us his story and helps us on our journey to discover who we are. Generous, insightful and genuinely helpful, this book will leave you wanting more.
—**Ian Galloway**, director of the Free Church Track and lecturer in leadership and mission, Cranmer Hall, Durham University

Nothing captures today's cultural zeitgeist more profoundly than the claim 'I identify as . . .'. Drawing on his own journey of godly formation of sexual attractions and desires, Andrew skilfully introduces his readers to some of the complex questions of identity and personal meaning. Firmly rooted in Christ, he points us to a deeper and more solid foundation for our sense of self.
—**Glynn Harrison** MD, retired consultant psychiatrist and emeritus professor of Psychiatry

Andrew explains clearly the flaws present and the difficulties experienced when a person allows their inner self and/or the ever-changing societal expectations to define who they are. There is, however, hope for the individual. In receiving their identity based on God's design and purpose, explains Andrew, the believer can acknowledge, address and even resolve how they are feeling without straying from the solid understanding of who they are. In an increasingly confused world, this short book is a treasure that should be studied and discussed by every church youth group and Sunday school class.
—**Jeannette Howard**, speaker and author of *Dwelling in the Land: Bringing Same-Sex Attraction Under the Lordship of Christ*

In *Finding Your Best Identity*, Andrew Bunt explores the power our core identity – or controlling self-understanding – has over us. He shows how both traditional and modern identities are unstable and ultimately crush us when we fail. Only our God-given relationship with Jesus provides an identity that is not fragile and that allows honesty and vulnerability without shame. It's an identity that cannot be taken away by changing experience, by the opinion of others or even by death itself. While Andrew explores these competing identities in conversation with sexuality and gender, this is a book that will benefit any current or potential follower of Jesus.

—**Greg Johnson**, pastor of Memorial Presbyterian Church in St. Louis, USA and author of *Still Time to Care: What We Can Learn from the Church's Failed Attempt to Cure Homosexuality*

With radical openness, personal experience, sensitivity and grace, Andrew approaches this minefield of a topic with one clear aim in mind: to help all people. The clarity here is vivid. The counsel here is godly. The freedom offered is persuasive. For all who want to be fully known and fully loved, this will point you in the right direction of true identity.

—**Tope Koleoso**, lead pastor, Jubilee Church London

This is a much-needed book in a society where there is such overwhelming pressure to look inside ourselves and discover our true identities. It is a book I wish I could have read as a young adult – I wrestled with doubts and questions about who I was until I realised that I am who God says I am and that he rejoices over me with singing!

—**Julie Maxwell**, community paediatrician and member of the General Synod

Andrew has written a book on identity that is concise, clear and practical. Whilst he applies his arguments particularly to matters of sexuality and gender, the principles in the book would be of great value to every person made in the image of God. Andrew provides a strong but easily understood critique of how our culture constructs identity. He then argues persuasively that a God-given identity frees us from the insecurity and pressure of letting either other people or our own feelings decide who we are.

—**Stuart Parker**, True Freedom Trust

There is no more important question in contemporary culture than 'Who am I?' Andrew Bunt tackles this head on, by asking the essential, deeper question 'How would I know?' He draws movingly on his own experience, and engages both with issues in popular culture and the reality of established research to address the question gently but directly. The result is truly impressive – a persuasive, compassionate and life-giving answer that will help so many. Take and read!

—**Ian Paul**, associate minister, St Nicholas' Church, Nottingham; adjunct professor of New Testament, Fuller Theological Seminary

With refreshing honesty, Andrew writes as someone who has walked through dark valleys whilst questioning his own identity. His reflections will help anyone facing similar struggles; they are a roadmap to guide us out of shame and confusion, and towards our Creator's good intention for each one of us.

—**Mark Pickering**, CEO of the Christian Medical Fellowship

'Who am I?' is one of the fundamental questions humans ask. Where we look for our answers is one of the most important decisions we can make. In this helpful, hopeful little book, Andrew helps us evaluate the possible options, and gives some practical, biblical advice on how to experience our best identity.

—**Jennie Pollock**, author of *If Only: Finding Joyful Contentment in the Face of Lack and Longing*

If you are struggling with your identity or know someone who is, this book will help you. Andrew writes with great honesty, clarity and understanding. If you are wrestling in your personal or public life with these realities or issues, I think you will read with increasing relief and gratitude. Two scriptures kept coming to mind 'In your light, we see light' (Psalm 36:9) and 'You will know the truth and the truth will set you free' (John 8:32).

—**Keith Sinclair**, national director, Church of England Evangelical Council

Andrew Bunt is quickly becoming one of my favorite writers on sexuality and gender, and this new book did not disappoint! Andrew combines biblical precision with pastoral compassion as he addresses two fundamental questions: Who are we? and How do we know? We live in a world where a myriad of voices and influences are trying to tell us who we are. Andrew graciously navigates us through the confusion and offers a theologically compelling case for finding our best identity—one that actually leads to human flourishing.

—**Preston Sprinkle**, Ph.D., president of The Center for Faith, Sexuality & Gender

Compassionate and compelling, insightful and instructive, Andrew Bunt's excellent book sheds light and brings clarity to a subject often distorted by emotion and conflict. Few things are more important than establishing your true identity. I urge you not only to read it but to help others by recommending it to them.

—**Terry Virgo**, founder of Newfrontiers and author of *God's Treasured Possession*

FINDING YOUR BEST IDENTITY

A short Christian introduction to identity,
sexuality and gender

Andrew Bunt

INTER-VARSITY PRESS
36 Causton Street, London SW1P 4ST, England
Email: ivp@ivpbooks.com
Website: www.ivpbooks.com

First published in 2022

British Library Cataloguing-in-Publication Data
A catalogue record for this book is available from the British Library.

ISBN: 978–1–78974–420–0
eBook ISBN: 978–1–78974–421–7

10 9 8 7 6 5 4 3 2 1

Set in Minion Pro 11.5/14.75 pt
Typeset by Westchester Publishing Services

In memory of

Becky

An exceptional woman and
one of God's greatest gifts to me.

And to those who have helped me find
and experience my best identity:

Nat, Caner and Jo, Paul, Mark, Steve, Will and Paris.

Thank you for loving me until I started to
believe it might actually be true.

Contents

Foreword

In *Finding Your Best Identity*, Andrew shares brilliantly about the experience and truth behind being Christian and navigating questions of LGBTQI+ experience. He employs his gifts not just as a disciple of Jesus, but as a caring pastor and incisive teacher. Knowing Andrew myself has been a profound blessing, and in these pages you will discover the same. Andrew demonstrates that Jesus calls us to a way of deep sacrifice which leads through the grief and mystery of suffering into the awesome joy and glory of Jesus' resurrection. From this root, he distinguishes between a healthy, life-giving identity and an identity from the wrong, wayward root. Showing how not just to integrate but also to submit our human identities to Christ, Andrew also unpicks the false duality between the harmful erasure of sexual or gender identity and its total rulership over our lives. He invites us into the integration Jesus' presence provides in our lives, saving us from idols and reductionism, and the polarity of Christian faith and gay or trans identity that has been so harmful to religious LGBTQI+ people.

The concerns that preoccupied and nourished the greatest Christian minds and hearts were always pastoral. They emerged from the life of the local church. This book arrives at a place we can ask those most important questions: How do we know the real us? Where do we tether our identities when they seem to control us and keep us from God's best for our lives? What is our ultimate identity? How do I avoid deleting my identities but instead steward them faithfully? What is God's way for our human identities to become beautiful parts of our witness, not competing with Jesus as Lord as the one who leads and guides our lives? How can we find the pathway to our best identity?

Andrew Bunt demonstrates in this book that he is someone called to carry this precious and millennia-old legacy forward for today's church and world. A movement is rising all around the world among LGBTQI+ (or same-sex attracted and gender dysphoric) Christians who are not just telling their stories, but also teaching the church from them. This movement needs this particular concise and wise contribution to the task of facing the mystery of God, human sexuality and gender. Andrew is an essential voice in this exciting new move of the Spirit. He carries the Jesus-focused heart of truly orthodox, Spirit-filled, LGTBQI+ Christians in a uniquely inspiring, light-hearted and down-to-earth way. From his wisdom we are empowered to steward our bodies through the cross in a way which does not come from legalism but from the grace of Jesus Christ.

Through Andrew's fascinating life story, we are brought into these questions and given answers that take us beyond the platitudes and the sometimes-heavy complexity of these questions. We witness the intersection of both trans and gay identities in his life – a perspective that has rarely been repre-sented. He shows us, through deep pain but also joy, how he reconciled these parts of his life with his Christian faith so as to offer us the best possible way of configuring these identities. His writing reflects a theological maturity that does not fall prey to the ideologically idolatrous voices we often see rehashed around us in both society and the church. Such a posture is rare and of precious significance, not just for Christians but also for all people seeking to understand faith and what it is to be LGBTQI+. We live in a world and a church which desire to control what it looks like to navigate identity and faith, but Andrew points beyond this harmful control to a liberating, other third way.

With succinct detail and a winsomely accessible tone, Andrew invites us on a journey into the glory of the good news of Jesus for LGBTQI+ people. We come out of this book no longer looking at being LGBTQI+ as a curse or a heavy burden, but a place for this glory to break through into the world. This book is a rare treatment of the LGBTQI+ question which you won't want to miss. I have always found that the path God takes us on is never what we expect. But it really brings us joy. This book invites us onto the narrow but satisfying and hope-filled path of Jesus which does not compromise truth nor allow identities to become harmful dictators. Andrew invites us into the deepest possible joy and points to the only true anchor for our identity: knowing oneself loved by the holy God revealed in Jesus Christ.

David Bennett
Member of the Archbishop
of Canterbury's College of Evangelists
Author of *A War of Loves:*
The Unexpected Story of a Gay Activist Discovering Jesus
Doctoral candidate
at the University of Oxford in Theology and Ethics

1

Who am I?

Who am *I*?

'Who am I?' This has been a big question for me.

For a period in my childhood, I was convinced that I was a girl. Though externally I seemed to be a boy, and everyone thought I was a boy, I felt that internally I was a girl. I remember living with the fear that one day I would get pregnant (obviously this was before I was aware how these things work!) and then my big secret would be revealed. I quietly resigned myself to the fact I'd just have to live with my parents for the rest of my life and never get married. As I grew up, this feeling went away, but I remained uncomfortable as a man, never really feeling I fitted in, uncomfortable in all-male environments, and secretly wanting to be considered 'one of the girls'.

My teen years raised new questions about my identity. As puberty hit, new desires emerged, but they weren't desires for girls, as I might have expected; they were for guys. At first, I didn't really realize what was going on; I don't think I had any understanding that some people are same-sex attracted or gay. I kept quiet about these new desires for several years, and it was still a secret known to only a few by the time I reached my twenties.

But all through those years I was listening, trying to make sense of what I was experiencing. Judging by what some people said, it seemed that this was the worst thing possible, that these desires somehow made me a lesser person, and this all made me believe I should never tell anyone. But at the same time, others seemed to think these desires were the most important thing about me, that they were actually who I am. These people seemed to think I should declare to the world 'I'm gay' and that I should be sure to embrace and act on my desires to find my best life.

In my twenties, identity continued to be an issue. I was now an adult who had left home and was trying to find my way in adult life, but I was also becoming increasingly self-conscious. I began to find that just being on my own in public made me so uncomfortable that my face would involuntarily twitch. During these years, I had a few fairly major meltdowns as my mental health yo-yoed up and down. In the wake of one of these meltdowns, with the help of a counsellor, I discovered I was living with an identity of which I wasn't even aware. Deep down, the controlling self-understanding in my life was that I was a freak and a weirdo. I assumed that was what everyone thought of me, and so I assumed that was just who I was.

I've had to wrestle with the question, 'Who am I?' Am I how I feel inside? Not a woman but not really fully a man? Am I my sexual desires, a gay guy who needs a husband to be happy? Or am I what I instinctively assume other people think of me, a freak and a weirdo?

These have been uncomfortable questions to ask. At times they've been very painful to ask, but as I've done so, I've found there is a better answer to the question, 'Who am I?' I have found that my best identity isn't based on what I feel or desire inside, and it isn't based on what I assume other people think about me; my best identity is based on what my Creator says about me. God dictates my identity. And therefore, I will find my best life, not by embracing everything I find within or by listening to what I hear (or just assume) around me; I will find my best life by living out my God-given identity.

What is identity?

What do I mean when I talk about identity? As I'll use it in this book, identity is our controlling self-understanding. All of us live with a concept of who we really are and what we believe to be most fundamental and important about us. This is a self-understanding. It's how we understand our self.

And that self-understanding, even if it remains subconscious, impacts how we feel and how we live. Your self-understanding can be involved in giving you a sense that you have worth and value, or that you don't, and it can therefore have a big impact on your emotional and mental health. That's why having an unhealthy identity can be so harmful and can take us to very dark and painful places.

Your self-understanding will also often impact how you live. Sometimes that's because we want to live out an identity in order to display it to those around us and to experience our best life through doing so. At other times it'll be because we're trying to escape from an identity; we want to be someone else. Who you think you are influences how you live your life.

In these ways, our identity controls us; it impacts how we feel and how we live. That's why it's a *controlling* self-understanding.

Working with this definition, there are lots of things that are true of us that aren't our identity (things like our race and ethnicity, occupation, and history). Something that is true of us only becomes our identity when it becomes core to how we view ourselves and when it therefore begins to exert some control over us, affecting how we feel and how we live. Identity is our controlling self-understanding.

How do I find who I am?

Understanding what identity is helps us to see why it is so important. It shows us that it's right and good to ask the question 'Who am I?' But there's actually another question that needs to be asked before this, a question we rarely think to ask. That question is 'How do I find who I am?'

In asking 'Who am I?' we take for granted that we know how best to find our identity. But do we really? My own journey hasn't just been about finding out who I am; at different points, I've been pretty certain who I am: a girl in a boy's body, or a gay man, or a freak and a weirdo. In reality, the question I needed an answer to was 'How do I find who I am?' That's the question that helps us find our best identity. And we want to find our best identity because doing so, and living out that identity, will help us experience our best life. Getting this right is really important.

Over the next few chapters, we'll unmask some of the different ways that people find their identity, seeing which work and which don't, and looking for the best answer to the question 'How do I find who I am?' Once we've got that answer, we'll be in a better position to ask, 'Who am I?'

Identity, sexuality and gender

One of the reasons identity is so important is because of the way it intersects with two aspects of human existence that are important for all of us: sexuality and gender.

In times gone by, and sadly all too often still today, some people have been made to feel like freaks or in some way less than human because of their experience of sexuality or gender. Identities have been placed on LGBTQ+ people, branding them with labels such as degenerate or disgusting. Christians have played our part in this, both in the past and the present, and the Bible's teaching has been wrongly understood and applied, resulting in damaging and destructive identities being placed on LGBTQ+ people.

But the importance of identity in relation to sexuality and gender is also seen in a very different way. In modern Western society, both sexual orientation (our enduring pattern of sexual and romantic attraction and desires) and gender identity (our internal sense of gender) are considered to be core identities. Many believe that these internal experiences are who we are, and that they therefore need to be embraced and expressed in order to allow us to live our best life. Against this backdrop, the historic Christian sexual ethic is seen as offensive and intolerant because it seems to ask people to deny who they really are.

Gay people are asked to deny who they really are because the Christian sexual ethic says marriage and sex are to be reserved for lifelong unions of one man and one woman.

Trans people are asked to deny who they really are because the Christian ethic says that our bodies are determinative for our gender, and so we should live out the gender of our biological sex.

When Christians and non-Christians, and increasingly Christians and other Christians, clash on issues of sexuality and gender, it isn't just because we have different views on who we can have sex with (which we do) or, more importantly, because we have different views on what sex and marriage are about (which we do), it's also because we have different views on how to find our best identity.

We need to think about this. If we don't think about it, we won't be able to engage with the world around us. We might try to engage, but we'll be talking past each other because we'll be talking about different topics without even realizing it and we'll be unaware of the pain that some people are experiencing, some of which may have been caused by Christians.

We need to think about it so we can engage with young people in our churches and our families. Every day the world around them is telling them that sexuality and gender are identity issues. It's no wonder that many hear the Bible's teaching, believe that God is asking them or their friends to deny who they really are, and consequently reject it as unreasonable and unloving.

And we need to think about it so we can engage with ourselves. Sexuality and gender are real life issues for all of us, and all of us, in different ways and to different extents, will be surrounded by the message that our sexuality and gender are who we are.

We need to think about identity. Is there an answer to the destructive identities that have often been placed on LGBTQ+ people? Is it true that the historic Christian sexual ethic asks many of us to deny who we really are? Before we can answer these questions, we need to know how to find our best identity, and to know that, we need to first ask the question: 'How do I find who I am?'

Questions for reflection and discussion

- In what ways have you had to wrestle with the question 'Who am I?'
- Have you considered the question 'How do I find who I am?' before? Why might it be important to do so?
- How have you experienced or observed the intersection of identity with sexuality and gender in your own life, the lives of those around you, or the culture in which you live?
- Why is thinking about identity in relation to sexuality and gender so important?

2

'Others decide'

Who am I? For years I believed that I was a freak and a weirdo. That wouldn't have been how I would have described myself if you'd asked me who I was; for a long time, I wasn't even fully conscious I believed that. But deep down I did, and that belief had horrible effects on my life.

One of these was insecurity. In my friendships, I assumed the only reason I had any friends at all was because they felt sorry for me. They were the few people kind enough to take pity on this freak and weirdo and their kindness, or some sense of duty, led them to stick with me as a friend. This deep-rooted belief would often leave me feeling low. Ultimately, I didn't believe that anyone really liked or loved me; I didn't truly believe God did, and actually I didn't really even like myself.

Multiple seasons of depression led me to see a Christian counsellor. Among lots of other things, identity was one of the key topics we talked about. I gradually became aware of the self-understanding with which I was living. But when I first saw it, I didn't think it was the problem; I genuinely thought it was true. I still remember the response of the first friend with whom I shared my growing realization: 'What? I've literally never thought of you as any weirder than anyone else!' I could tell from the way they said this that they really meant it. I was genuinely shocked. 'People don't think I'm a freak and weirdo? Maybe I'm not.'

What had happened in all this? I'd allowed others to decide who I was. My sense of self was based on what (I thought) other people thought of me, and that sense of self was controlling me: my sense of worth and value – or rather, my lack of it – flowed from that self-understanding. And in this, I'd fallen foul of one of the great problems of letting other people decide who we are: we rarely really know what people think of us. But even if we do, is this a good way to find who we are?

Understanding 'others decide'

Many of us find our identity in this way. We base our sense of self on what people think of us, or rather what we think they think of us. That sense of self exerts control over us, and so it affects how we live, and it influences whether we feel we have worth and value.

This all starts with the assumption that there are a certain set of criteria by which people evaluate us. These criteria could be the rules or expectations of a community or the virtues recognized as necessary to qualify as a good or successful person. Sometimes they are articulated somewhere (perhaps in a law code), but often they are just the shared assumptions of a community or culture.

The important thing is that the criteria are something by which we can be evaluated. We can do a better or worse job of living up to them and that shapes how people think of us. In my case, I thought people were evaluating me against the unspoken criteria for being a 'normal' person. Most people do pretty well on these criteria; they're 'normal'. But in my mind, measured against them, I did badly, and so I was a freak and a weirdo.

In this way of making identity, the criteria are key. If we live up to them, people think well of us, and we get a healthy identity with a good sense of worth and value. But if we fail to live up to the criteria, people think badly of us, and we get an unhealthy identity and a low view of ourselves. Identity is therefore based on what we do. To have and maintain a healthy identity, we have to keep living up to the criteria.

'Others decide' in action

We can often spot this way of forming identity at work in the lives of celebrities. Being in the public eye is the perfect position in which to allow others to decide your identity. Madonna is a good example. In an interview with the *Guardian*, Madonna was asked what she had meant when, back in the 1980s, she had said she wanted to rule the world: 'I think I just meant I want to make a mark on the world, I want to be a somebody. Because I grew up feeling like a nobody.'[1] I'm sure many of us would relate to Madonna's wish: we want to be somebody, to be known, recognized, and thought well of. Perhaps we want people to consider us to be successful, intelligent, attractive or maybe just nice. And when they do, we feel good. It gives us a sense of worth and value. We're allowing others to decide who we are.

But it's not just fame that can make us susceptible to this way of finding identity. There are lots of ways we can allow others to decide who we are. It can happen with our work.

Many of us will be susceptible to looking to our jobs to find our worth and value. We want to have a good job and to be successful. If we're in education, perhaps school or university, it can happen with our academic achievements. We want to be top of the class or a high achieving student. How do these things give us worth and value? Because they make other people think well of us. If our job meets the unspoken criteria for a worthwhile or impressive career or if we are particularly successful in our job, people think well of us. If we get high marks and do well academically, people think well of us, they're impressed, they think we're a good person.

The same thing can happen in our relationships. We might not always spot it, but our relationship with a spouse or friend can become the most important thing to us and the place to which we look to be reassured that we're a good, lovable person. The relationship gives us our core sense of self and worth because the relationship proves that this person thinks well of us. They get to decide who we are.

Or it can happen just from a desire to be known as someone who is kind or generous. To be considered kind or generous requires living up to certain criteria. It is an identity that is based on our actions and our performance. If we do well, or at least make it look as if we're doing well, we receive a healthy identity as someone whom others recognize as kind or generous, and that will make us feel good about ourselves. But if we do badly, that identity can come crashing down and be replaced by an identity of someone who is unkind or ungenerous.

None of these things are bad in themselves. Both work and relationships are good gifts from God, and we should want to be people who are kind and generous, two qualities which reflect God's own heart. But while enjoying God's good gifts and seeking to become the people God wants us to be, we have to be careful not to allow the wrong things to become the source of our identity because allowing others to decide who we are isn't a good way to find our identity.

Evaluating 'others decide'

'Others decide' is a popular way to answer the question, 'How do I find who I am?' But it's also full of problems.

One big problem is that it *can easily create really unhealthy, destructive identities*. Madonna gives this away in the interview mentioned earlier. She wants to be somebody because she grew up feeling like a nobody. It sounds as if, as a child, she didn't believe people thought well of her and, therefore, she didn't have much of a sense of her own worth and value. 'Others decide' soon backfires when people don't think well of us, and none of us can escape having times when some people might think badly of us. When this happens, we're left without a sense of our own value and worth, and that can quickly have a negative effect on our mental health and wellbeing.

These unhealthy identities can arise because we do badly or make a big mistake. We've failed to fulfil the criteria of being a good person and so, if others are deciding who we are, we end up with a horrible identity – a bad person, or a failure or a freak. They can also arise because we wrongly assume that people think badly of us. We can't ever be sure what people think of us, so it's easy to assume that they think badly of us. Once we do, we will easily interpret all the available evidence through that lens, making it support that conclusion. Letting others decide who we are opens us up to the possibility of some very unpleasant and harmful identities.

But even if letting others decide does give us a healthy identity, there are still some problems.

First, letting others decide who we are *can create crushing insecurity*. If we can never really be completely sure what other people think of us, how can we be sure that their evaluation of us is a good one? How can we ever be sure we've done enough to make people think well of us? There can be no lasting security in an identity decided by others.

As well as insecurity, this also brings *incredible pressure*. If others' perspective on us is based on how well or badly we do according to a set of criteria, we have to be constantly living up to these criteria if we want to maintain a healthy identity. Ultimately, it's all based on our performance, and that puts huge pressure on us to keep up an act. Living this way is exhausting.

But perhaps most problematic, *an identity where others decide who we are is unstable*: at any moment a good identity can be lost if we make a mistake or fail to live up to the criteria.

If you root your identity in your academic achievements, what happens if you have a few bad weeks and you're no longer the star student? If you root your identity in a relationship and what it tells you about yourself, what happens if you have a big argument or even if the relationship comes to an end? If your sense of worth comes from being a kind person, what happens when you have a bad day and people no longer think you're so kind?

Even if allowing others to decide who we are gives us a healthy identity for a time, that identity is always inherently unstable because we can't guarantee we'll always live up to the criteria and we aren't always in control of what people think of us.

'Others decide' doesn't seem to be a very good answer to the question, 'How do I find who I am?'

Sexuality and gender

How is this all relevant to questions of sexuality and gender? One key way is in the reality of LGBTQ+ shame.

Shame is a sense of embarrassment, discomfort or humiliation about an aspect of oneself, and it is a huge issue among LGBTQ+ people. It is likely that shame is one of the factors lying behind the disproportionately high rates of mental health problems and addictions among LGBTQ+ people.[2]

British singer-songwriter Will Young is just one famous figure who has talked about his own experience of shame and its impact on him.

[S]hame is certainly something that LGBT people experience in bucketloads. From day dot the message from the powers that be is that we are wrong, less than human, freaks. To be gay at school is the ultimate crushing accusation, it brings about segregation and social exclusion in the extreme. We feel unsafe in the world and we have to be on guard in the playground, at home and merely walking the streets . . . [I]s it any wonder that LGBT people's mental health is far more at risk than that of heterosexuals? How can one exist with such deep soul-wounding? We internalize this pain and turn it onto ourselves, leading to excruciating shame and internalized homophobia against ourselves and our brothers and sisters.[3]

These words capture well the experience of LGBTQ+ shame, and it's not hard to see in them how this shame is an example of others deciding who we are. It's a view that comes from someone else ('the powers that be'). It evaluates us according to some unspoken criteria ('we are wrong, less than human, freaks'). And though it starts as the evaluation of others, it soon makes its way into us and becomes the way we view ourselves ('we internalize . . . and turn it onto ourselves').

Many – maybe even most – LGBTQ+ people will have their own stories of being made to feel that they are less than human or freaks because of how others have evaluated them.

I do. As a child, long before I even knew I was same-sex attracted, peers jested that I would grow up to be 'a gay politician'. This wasn't a compliment about my abilities; it was a joke about my difference. Not long after, I overheard a trusted older woman talking to her husband about a historical figure who was gay, saying, 'Doesn't it make you think less of him to know he was like that?' By this point I was becoming aware of my same-sex attraction, and I made a mental note that people would think less of me if they knew about it. At secondary school, I was regularly the butt of a supposed joke where a guy would pretend to have a crush on me and to hit on me. (He's since come out as gay himself. Sometimes a person's way of dealing with gay shame is to take part in the jokes.) When I moved to a new town at eighteen, I noticed that a group of new friends regularly referred to things they didn't like as 'gay'. Clearly 'gay' was not good.

The fact I was different had always been pretty clear to me. No one had to tell me that. The fact that that difference somehow made me less than other people was something I learnt from these kinds of experiences.

We might like to think that this doesn't still happen today, but it does. In 2019, a survey of 1,000 teachers found that homophobic bullying is more common in UK schools than bullying related to either race, sex or religion. Seventy-one per cent of the teachers had witnessed homophobic bullying, 35% saying they see it occur at least once a month.[4] A 2017 survey of over 5,000 LGBT people living in Great Britain found that almost one in five had experienced negative comments or conduct from work colleagues because of their sexuality or gender identity.[5] The same survey found that three in five transgender students in British universities and more than one in five LGB students had experienced the same from their peers.[6] The statistics are shocking, but the stories are even more heartbreaking.

I had a customer threatening violence and calling me a faggot repeatedly while at work. There were multiple times where people call [sic] me a fag under their breath too.[7]

I was walking to the university library when a group of young people started yelling things at me like "oh look at this dyke", "you look like a man . . . wait, is that the point, you tranny?" as I walked past.[8]

It's even more heartbreaking to realize that we, as Christians, have often been vocal among the voices contributing to LGBTQ+ shame. Half of my own experiences related above were in Christian contexts. Many people have experienced far worse, being led to believe that God hates them and that they are an abomination.

What does all this reveal? First it reveals a problem that needs to be addressed, and it's a problem that Christians should be at the forefront of addressing.

To make LGBTQ+ people feel that they are of less value than others or that they are not loved by God is not the way of Jesus. In Jesus, we find the beautiful combination of an unswerving commitment to God's standards and an equally strong commitment to expressing God's love. Jesus never allowed people to think that sin was acceptable, but he also never allowed people to believe that God didn't or couldn't love them. When Jesus encountered those who would most have experienced shame in his culture – tax collectors, prostitutes and lepers – he didn't reject them or shame them; he talked to them, ate with them, offered help to them, and loved them. If we are the followers of Jesus, we should be doing the same to those who experience shame today.

But LGBTQ+ shame also reveals some of the key problems with allowing others to dictate our identity. This way of finding who we are can easily lead to unhealthy and destructive identities because we don't always live up to people's criteria, and so people don't always think well of us.

We might question whether their criteria or their evaluation of us is correct – and in this case it would certainly be right to do so – but as long as we're allowing others to decide who we are, we'll find it hard to avoid the negative effects of this kind of evaluation. We need a better way of finding who we are.

Am I a freak and a weirdo?

I've come to realize that most people don't think of me as a freak and a weirdo. But the opinion of others still isn't a good basis for my identity. They might not think that of me now, but they could in the future. Even if allowing others to decide my identity might give me a healthy identity for now, there's no guarantee it always will. If 'others decide' isn't a good answer to the question 'How do I find who I am?' perhaps we should try a different answer.

Questions for reflection and discussion

- Where do you see an 'others decide' approach to identity at work in the world around you?
- In what areas of life are you susceptible to letting the evaluation of other people shape your sense of self?
- Have you experienced or observed any of the problems that can come from an 'others decide' approach to forming identity?
- Is LGBTQ+ shame something of which you have been aware before? What's your experience or understanding of it?

3

'I decide'

Who am I? Lots of people think that I am my sexuality. I'm a guy who's attracted to guys and so I'm gay. And being gay, it seems, is the most important thing about me. It's the real me, and I need to accept that and express that in order to be truly happy. Because I'm gay, I need a boyfriend or at least I just need to be having sex with men in order to find true satisfaction.

That's what the world around me seems to think. I get told it every time a new celebrity comes out as gay. They're now being true to themselves. They're now finally able to live their best life. Those who have already entered into a relationship often talk about it being the final step to embracing who they really are. The same message comes across in films and TV shows. A character starts in some level of distress. They come to accept that they are gay; they embrace their experience as who they really are, find a partner, and all their problems are solved. They're being true to themselves, and that allows them to enjoy their best life.

Sometimes these sorts of things make me stop and think. Is this who I am? Is the most important thing about me that I'm a gay man? Do I need a boyfriend or a husband to find my best life? Apparently so.

But when people tell me that I am my sexuality, they're not actually telling me who I am; they're telling me how to find who I am. How do I find who I am according to this view? I decide. I look inside, I find or choose who I am, and I then proclaim that to the world around me. Maybe this is a better way of finding who I am.

Understanding 'I decide'

In modern Western culture, 'I decide' is a very popular answer to the question 'How do I find who I am?'

It rests on the idea that what is inside us is the most important thing about us. Anything external – our bodies, other people, traditions, religions – is less important and can be trumped by what's inside. And so, to find who we are, we have to look inside.

Often, we look inside at our feelings – what we intuitively 'feel' to be true – or our desires. What is it that we want? What is it that we feel will make us truly happy? These things are then embraced as who we really are.

Sometimes, though, identity isn't discovered at all; it's just created. Some people will decide their own identity, not based on what they feel or desire, but simply based on their own choice. 'This is who I am because it's who I say I am.'

In this way of making identity, all that matters is what the individual thinks and says of themselves. Nothing outside of the person can dictate who they are, and so anything outside that seeks to challenge or change how they view themselves or to stop them from embracing and expressing what they find inside, is considered oppressive and harmful. Only the individual can know who they are, and so only they can tell the rest of us, and no one and nothing else can change or challenge that identity.

'I decide' in action

This way of forming identity can be seen all around us. It lies behind many of the popular, inspirational slogans we see pasted across the internet.

Always stay true to yourself and never sacrifice who you are for anyone.

Never change who you are because someone else has a problem with it.

They might not state it explicitly, but these sorts of statements are usually interpreted as meaning that only we can decide who we are; it doesn't matter what other people think, and if they don't like who we are, they're the ones with a problem, not us. I decide. Nothing else matters.

We can also find this idea in the background to many elements of popular culture. The great heroes of our day are those who embrace who they feel themselves to be, while bravely ignoring the oppressive voices who might challenge that perception.

You can often spot this in song lyrics. There are many examples, but absolute classics are songs like *I Am What I Am*, made famous by Gloria Gaynor. Look up the lyrics. You'll see the message is easy to spot. Who am I? I'm whoever I say I am – the me I create. And it doesn't matter what other people say, whether they praise me or whether they pity me. This is who I am, and I'm not going to apologize for that.

Another classic is Diana Ross' *I'm Coming Out*. Who am I? I'm the me who has been trapped inside, my wants and my abilities, and now I've got tell the world because they need to know the real me who's inside, and the only way they can know that is if I reveal myself. I decide who I am. And you can only know who I am if I tell you.

And it's not only in songs that we can see this idea. It's also prominent in TV and films.[1] The classic example from my childhood was the film, *Babe*. Babe is an orphaned piglet who ends up on a farm trying to work out who he is and where he fits in. As time goes on, he realizes that, though externally he's a pig, inside he feels like he should be a sheepdog, and so Babe embraces and expresses that identity and ends up winning a sheepherding competition. Babe is the hero we all cheer for because he looks at who he is inside, and he embraces and expresses that identity, even in the face of challenge and ridicule from others.

But the clearest example (and, I'll be honest, a film I love) is Disney's *Frozen*. Elsa is one of the great heroes of our time because she bravely embraces and expresses what she finds inside – her magical powers – in defiance of the attempts of others to have her hide these powers and deny who she really is. And it's clear that while Elsa's self-suppression leads to damage and destruction, in the form of an eternal winter for Arendelle, her self-expression brings freedom and flourishing in the saving of Arendelle and the new age of open doors at the palace. Clearly, who we are inside is what is most important about us, and denying or supressing that will only cause damage to ourselves and others.

And all of this is perfectly encapsulated in the film's most famous song, *Let It Go*. No doubt one of the reasons this song was such a huge phenomenon was because it expresses the experience of the quintessential hero of our culture.

Let It Go starts with Elsa's internal experience which she has tried to keep hidden but is just too strong for it to remain inside. Up until this point she's been allowing others to decide who she is. She's been 'the good girl' who has kept her powers hidden, meeting the criteria set by her parents and others around her.

Now, though, it's all become too much, and it's time to let it all out. The cry of 'Let it go' is a bold and defiant choice to throw off the oppressive expectations of others and embrace who she really is inside. She's no longer letting others decide who she is. Now she gets to decide, and she's letting the world see the true her who has been hiding inside. The song ends with Elsa having thrown off the shackles of an oppressive identity given to her by others. She stands proudly in the light with utter disdain for those who had previously oppressed her, those who wanted her to be a good girl, and with confident disregard for the consequences of her actions.

Evaluating 'I decide'

'I decide' is a popular way of answering the question 'How do I find who I am?' And it's an answer we're being told all the time by the culture around us. On the surface it sounds great: wouldn't it be great if we were all free to decide who we are with no one challenging or oppressing us? And wouldn't it be great if we could just embrace and express whatever we find inside with no one holding us back or criticizing us? It sounds like the vision of a great world, and it's a world some people are actively working towards.

But would that world really be as great as it might first seem? Does 'I decide' work as a way of finding a solid, static, life-giving identity? I'm not sure it does.

A big problem with 'I decide' is that it puts *huge pressure* on us. In this way of finding identity, only we can really know who we are, and only we can tell others who we are. That means it's something we have to do on our own. No one can do it for us. We're left on our own to make one of the biggest and most life-impacting decisions possible. That's a lot of pressure, especially as deciding who we are is not always straightforward.

The impact of this pressure is particularly noticeable among teenagers. Perhaps you're a teenager and you can relate to this. The world around you is constantly telling you that you must be true to yourself and that only you can know who you really are. Maybe you feel anxious because you're not sure who you are and you're afraid that you might miss your best life. You know no one else can tell you who you are, so your happiness is on your shoulders. That's a lot to carry. 'I decide' identity puts huge pressure on us. When we realize this, rather than sounding freeing or life-giving, deciding our own identity begins to sound stressful.

Part of this stress is because sometimes, when we look inside, we might find that things *aren't very clear*. We might find feelings and desires that conflict. How do we know which one is the real us and which one we should therefore embrace and express to allow us to experience our best life? What if I really want a relationship with someone who lives in California, but I also really want a job that's based in London? Which desire should I embrace to be true to myself and to find my best life?

And sometimes we struggle even to know what we actually want or feel. One of the many online articles offering advice on how to find our true self points out that 'it can be easy to confuse what is *actually* you and what you *think* is you'.[2] We can struggle to even accurately assess what's inside us. Deciding our own identity isn't straightforward, and that can make it stressful.

And if we do find conflicting desires, on what basis do we make the decision as to which one constitutes the real us? The stakes are high; knowing who we really are is important, but what can help us to make that decision? One of the problems with 'I decide' is that it creates identities that are *unsupported*. There's no authority we can appeal to in order to help us choose between competing desires, because nothing outside of us should have a say in our identity. The decision lies with us, our own choice.

We also know that our feelings and desires can change. An identity built on them is *inherently unstable.* If I look back and think of the different things I have wanted to do as a job, I quickly realize how much desires can change. At different points in my life, I have wanted to be an Egyptologist, an airport worker, a schoolteacher, a musician and a West End musical director. (I'm still quite keen on that last one, but sadly it's not going to happen!) Our desires are anything but stable.

Some might think this doesn't matter, but it increases the pressure on us. Not only do we have to find who we are, we have to keep checking that we're still who we have previously decided we are, and then if we find that we have changed, we have to decide on our identity again. A failure to do so would be a failure to be true to ourselves, resulting in the forfeiting of our best life. But trying to keep up with our changing desires is exhausting. If I believed that my desires to do different jobs revealed who I am and if I followed those desires as the route to my best life, I would have exhausted myself trying to change careers so many times. Not only does 'I decide' put us under pressure, it puts us under ongoing pressure. If you follow 'I decide', you can never rest, content in your settled identity, because it's always liable to change.

A world where we all decided our own identities would put us all under a lot of pressure, but it would also allow identities that often cause *unintended harm*. Core to this approach to identity formation is that it pays no attention to anything outside of us, rather what's outside has to adapt to accommodate our self-defined identity. The right to decide who we are therefore trumps any negative consequences that the decision might have for other people.

So, if someone decides that core to who they are is an entrepreneurial spirit and a deep need to succeed in business, they might build their whole life around their work. Everything they have – time, money, energy – will go into their business. And why shouldn't it? They're just being true to themselves after all. But what about the impact on their friends or their spouse or their children? They might well become the unintended victims of this person embracing who they've decided they are.

And maybe that points us towards what might be the biggest problem with 'I decide' as a way of finding who we really are. An 'I decide' identity is *ultimately inconsistent* because the approach can't be applied universally. We can all recognize that there might be times when we look inside ourselves and find feelings and desires that are not good and that we would not say are who we are. We wouldn't encourage someone with such desires to embrace and express them as their true self, and if someone acted on such desires, we wouldn't celebrate them or even excuse them as brave self-expression. The same is true of identities that some people create for themselves regardless of what they feel inside. There are plenty of identities almost all of us would agree are not acceptable.

What happens if I look inside myself and find a deep desire to kill lots of people, or if I just decide that who I am is a blood-thirsty murderer? Can I follow my desires or embrace my self-created identity and do what I want? Will I be celebrated as someone who is bravely expressing my true self even in the face of challenge or criticism from others? I expect not.[3]

In which case, 'I decide' isn't such good news because it doesn't really work. None of us really believe that who we are inside or who we say we are is always who we really are. It seems, in reality, we look inside and pick out the feelings or desires that our culture tells us are constitutive of identity. In that case, it's no longer 'I decide'; it's become 'culture decides'.

This is a problem that secular thinkers have spotted. In an article titled 'Just Be True To Yourself? Not Quite', biophilosopher and social science researcher Dr Jeremy Sherman, writes:

> Being true to oneself can't be defined by what we think someone's true self should be. Though I think he's about as loathsome as a person can be, I'd say Trump is being true to himself.
>
> That's the problem with being true to yourself as a universal rule. Hitler was true to himself. So was Martin Luther King. We like MLK's authenticity but not Hitler's. Why? Because we like MLK's true self.[4]

No one really believes that everyone should be able to choose their own identity or to embrace and express everything they find inside.

So, since it puts us under incredible pressure and no one is really prepared to fully believe it, maybe 'I decide' isn't the best answer to the question, 'How do I find who I am?'

Sexuality and gender

An 'I decide' approach to identity is a key feature of modern Western beliefs about sexuality and gender. Both sexual orientation (our enduring pattern of sexual and romantic attraction and desires) and gender identity (our internal sense of gender) are viewed as core identities. Because of this, embracing and expressing our sexual orientation and gender identity are considered vital steps to enjoying our best life.

It's not hard to spot this in the world around us. The language of identity permeates discussions of sexuality and gender. One place it is often most evident is in celebrity coming out stories.

One of the most prominent coming out stories in recent years was that of Philip Schofield, the popular TV presenter who came out as gay on ITV's *This Morning* in February 2020.[5] The feature on *This Morning* and responses to it demonstrate how deeply ingrained the idea of sexuality as identity is in our culture. At one point Schofield expressed his feelings of guilt about the impact his coming out would have on his wife and children. But co-presenter Holly Willoughby was quick to reassure him, 'You can't change who you are.' This is who Schofield is and so, even if it might hurt other people, he's got to embrace and express his desires.

While some people on social media picked up on the impact on Schofield's family, many seemed to share the idea that Schofield's sexuality is who he is. Some of these responses were from famous figures: David Walliams, for example, tweeted, 'Let's hope we are moving towards a world where no one has to come out anymore, they can just be *who they are* and celebrate that.'[6] Members of the public also added their support:

> I think your [sic] really brave and strong minded to have come out and finally be at peace with *who you truly are.*[7]

> Take each day at a time . . . You are lucky to have the support . . . Be *who you are* . . .[8]

> Very brave to come out Phillip. To hide *who you are* for all them years must of [sic] been awful.[9]

Schofield's announcement wasn't just understood as an update about part of his life. It was understood as a declaration of who he is at the core of his being and was accompanied by the belief that embracing and expressing that identity would be vital for Schofield to find his best life.

The same ideas are often applied to gender identity. In September 2019, singer Sam Smith took to Instagram to announce that they had decided to change their pronouns, but this wasn't just a matter of personal preference, it was a declaration of who they really are:

'I've decided I am changing my pronouns to THEY/ THEM ♡ after a lifetime of being at war with my gender *I've decided to embrace myself for who I am . . .* I understand there will be many mistakes and mis gendering but all I ask is you please please try. *I hope you can see me like I see myself now.*'[10]

For Smith, who they are is what they find inside, and so the only way we can know who they are is if they tell us. Now that they've done that, the hope is that we too will see their true identity.

The personal nature of identity formation in our culture was also highlighted in a Starbucks advertising campaign in 2020. The #whatsyourname campaign drew on Starbucks' practice of writing a customer's name on their cup and the way this gives transgender and gender-diverse people an opportunity to decide their own identity: 'We discovered that they found Starbucks stores to be a safe space, where their new name was accepted, and they could be recognized as *who they are*.'[11] What we feel inside or who we say we are, is who we are.

But while widely accepted, the application of 'I decide' to sexuality and gender isn't without its problems. Several of the weaknesses of 'I decide' come to the fore in examples in the world around us.

Schofield's coming out highlights the pressure that 'I decide' can put us under. Some of this pressure is created by the fact that such an approach to identity can leave us unclear on who we are. In expressing guilt about the impact on his wife and children, Schofield reveals that there are competing desires in him. There are romantic and sexual desires for men, but there's also a desire to love and protect his family. Which of these desires should be embraced to find who he is? It seems he's opted to favour his sexual orientation over his desire to protect his family, but why? What authority says that that's the right choice between the two? It's an identity that's unsupported by any authority. And, of course, in acknowledging the impact on his wife and children, Schofield is revealing that 'I decide' identities often produce unintended victims.

Sexuality and gender as core identities also remind us that 'I decide' can create identities that are 'unstable'. Our sexual desires, which many of us might assume are fairly static, are actually often not as static as we think. An increasing amount of research is demonstrating the reality of sexual fluidity among both men and women.[12] Sexual orientation is not always a stable basis for identity.

Some may think that this doesn't matter. But if we build our identity on our experience of sexuality and that experience is liable to change, we are put in the stressful position of having to constantly monitor whether we are still who we have previously concluded we are. And perhaps more problematically, the unstable nature of such an identity is likely to create unintended victims: what if I follow my desires into a committed relationship with someone of the opposite sex, but later find that my sexuality changes and I feel more attracted to people of the same sex. Does that new identity justify my abandoning the commitment I have made to my opposite-sex partner so I can be true to who I now am?

The same problem of fluidity can be seen in relation to gender identity. A *Guardian* article reporting the words of four young people who identify as non-binary includes the story of River, an eighteen-year-old from Portugal. River tells us, 'I haven't come out to my family. My family's supportive, but I'm scared to tell them about it [in case] in a couple of years I don't feel like calling myself non-binary any more [sic] and I have to do the whole thing again.'[13] River recognizes the problem of an identity that can change. The instability of an identity found inside has left this eighteen-year-old not even feeling comfortable to talk to their own family about their experience. That doesn't sound very life-giving; it sounds stressful.

And we can also see evidence that an 'I decide' identity is ultimately inconsistent. The common cultural narrative tells us that our sexual desires are core to who we are: we are our sexual orientation, and therefore we must embrace and express those desires to find our best life. However, we all recognize that there are some sexual desires we could experience about which we would not say this.[14] It would seem we're not always able to be consistent in an 'I decide' approach.

When it comes to gender, in other situations where there is a clash between the objective realities of the physical body and the subjective self-perception of an individual, most of us would not view an individual's internal sense of self as a good basis for that person's identity. Examples here would be situations where people feel themselves to be of another species or able-bodied people who feel they should be disabled.[15] There's no doubt that these experiences can be genuine, but few of us would agree that they constitute who someone really is. Again, it seems we struggle to be consistent in applying an 'I decide' approach across the board.

Am I my sexuality?

'I decide' is a very popular answer to the question, 'How do I find who I am?' But it doesn't seem to be a very good answer. There's no doubt that I am attracted to people of the same sex, just as there's no doubt that some people feel themselves to be of a different gender to that suggested by their bodily sex, but neither sexual orientation nor gender identity are a good basis for identity. That suggests they aren't who we are, and so embracing and expressing them isn't vital to experience our best life. But that still leaves us needing to know who we are so we can live out our best identity. If 'others decide' doesn't work, and 'I decide' doesn't work, we need to look at another answer to our key question.

Questions for reflection and discussion

- Where do you see an 'I decide' approach to identity at work in the world around you?
- What elements of your internal life are you susceptible to letting define you?
- Have you experienced or observed any of the problems that can come from an 'I decide' approach to forming identity?
- Is the view that sexual orientation and gender identity are core identities something of which you have been aware? What's your experience of this perspective?

4

'God decides'

So, who am I? Allowing other people to decide who I am doesn't work and deciding for myself who I am doesn't work. I still need a way of finding who I am that will give me a solid, static, life-giving identity. There must be another, better answer to the question, 'How do I find who I am?' And thankfully, there is. It's not 'others decide' and it's not 'I decide'; it's 'God decides'.

Our best identity is found when we allow our controlling self-understanding to be determined by our relationship with our Creator and what he says about us on the basis of that relationship. The most life-giving form of identity we can have within this reality is Christian identity: an identity we receive as we enter into relationship with God based on the work of Christ. This is the identity that can give us the best true and lasting sense of worth and value, and it's by living out this identity that we can experience our best life.

In my own struggles with identity, understanding and experiencing Christian identity has been truly life changing. Recognizing that I am who God says I am, based on what Christ has done, has freed me from the destructive impact of the alternative identities I had been living with. It offered me a way out from the perfectionism and the fear of failure that had come to enslave me because I was so concerned about what people thought of me – they, after all, were the ones who were getting to decide who I am. Christian identity replaced my inability to believe that I am really loved with the certain knowledge that I am and will always be loved, regardless of how perfectly or imperfectly I do things and whether I'm successful or not. It also freed me from the worry that I needed to embrace my sexual desires as who I am in order to find true fulfilment, and the accompanying fear that if I did that, I might then never find someone to help me enact that identity in a loving relationship. Knowing that my best life can only be found by embracing and living out my identity as a child of God has helped me to acknowledge the unquestionable reality of my sexuality, but to not be controlled by it.

There was a time when I couldn't look myself in the mirror and say that I am fearfully and wonderfully made and when I couldn't really believe that anyone loved me. Now I could look you in the eye and tell you that I am God's workmanship, created in Christ, and that I am both fully known and fully loved. God has radically changed me, and that's all because I've come to realize that the best way to truly find who I am is to remember: God decides.

Understanding 'God decides'

In 'God decides', our identity is rooted in what God says about us on the basis of our position in relation to him. We take hold of what God says about us and we allow that to shape our sense of self, which in turn impacts how we feel and live.

'God decides' identity is received. It stands in contrast to 'others decide' in which identity is achieved through the actions we perform. And it also stands in contrast to 'I decide' in which identity is either discovered within or created through personal choice. In 'God decides', it doesn't matter what other people think about us and it doesn't matter how we feel or who we'd like to be; all that matters is who God says we are. His is the voice we listen to and allow to shape our self-understanding. This identity then becomes the basis on which we can experience a sense of worth and value.

In Scripture, we see this approach to identity illustrated in the life of Jesus. Jesus didn't allow the evaluation of other people to determine his sense of self or worth. And he didn't seek to discover or create his identity for himself. He knew who he was, and this identity was rooted in his relationship to God the Father. Even at the age of twelve, Jesus knew who he was, despite the fact his earthly parents didn't (Luke 2:49–50), and this identity was confirmed by divine declarations at his baptism (Mark 1:11) and at the Transfiguration (Mark 9:7). It was this identity which formed the basis for how Jesus lived (John 5:19). It gave him a solid, secure sense of his worth and his value.

And what we see in the life of Jesus is also what we see throughout Scripture. The fact that our identity is best rooted in our relationship to God is so fundamental to the worldview of the Bible that it is never explicitly stated; it is just assumed throughout.[1]

'God decides' in action

So, what is the identity we receive from God through our relationship with him? Well, the Bible actually talks about two levels of identity from God: human identity and Christian identity.

Human identity

For all humans, one form of relationship we have with God, and a core part of our God-given identity, is as a bearer of his image. All humans, regardless of age, status, race, sexual orientation or gender identity, are created in God's image. This is one of the very first things Scripture teaches us about ourselves:

> So God created man in his own image,
> in the image of God he created him;
> male and female he created them. (Genesis 1:27)

The image of God speaks of a family likeness between us and God. We see this in Genesis 5:3:

> When Adam had lived 130 years, he fathered a son in his own likeness, after his image, and named him Seth.

Adam's son Seth is in the likeness and image of Adam. There is a family resemblance: like father, like son. In the same way, we are in God's likeness and image. There is a family resemblance: like God, like human. Scripture doesn't specify the exact form of this likeness, but it's an identity that is true nonetheless.

The image of God is an identity that is given to us. It isn't dependent on what other people think or how we feel; it rests purely on how we stand in relation to God – as those who resemble him. And it's an identity that is static and stable. Nothing we do and nothing that is done to us, nothing we feel and nothing we desire, can change the truth that we bear God's image.[2]

And this identity is hugely important. It's because we are created in the image of God that every human life has incredible value and dignity and is worthy of honour and respect. The image of God is the reason why human life should be protected (Gen. 9:5–6) and why even cursing other people is inappropriate (James 3:9–10). It is therefore the reason why we should stand up against discrimination, injustice and abuse, and why we should work for equality and justice for all people.

The image of God also points towards the place where we as humans can find our best life. As those created in God's image, we are made for relationship with him. And that leads us to the second level of identity from God.

Christian identity

While the image of God is an immovable foundation for human identity, it alone doesn't solve all of our identity problems. A second level of our identity rests not on our likeness to God but on our personal relationship with him. On this level we can have a bad identity or a good identity.

All of us start with a bad identity because all of us start in rebellion against God. As those who have failed in our obligations to our Creator (Rom. 1:18–23), we are ungodly, sinners, enemies of God (Rom. 5:6, 8, 10). Far from being children of God, we are children of wrath (Eph. 2:3). This is bad news (to put it mildly!).

But it's against this background that the gospel comes as good news. The gospel is good news because it offers us a new, secure, life-giving identity. In the gospel we can find the solution to all our crises of identity.

Through the gospel, we are forgiven and reconciled to God. And as our relationship with God is transformed, so is our identity: enemies become friends (John 15:14), sinners become saints (Rom. 1:7) and children of wrath become children of God (Rom. 8:14–16; 1 Peter 1:14; 1 John 3:1).

And this identity is secure, static and unchanging because of what it's based on. Christian identity stands on the work of Christ. It is because of Christ's perfect life and sacrificial death that our relationship with God can be transformed. As Christians, God relates to us based, not on what we have done or do, how we feel or what we desire, but purely on what Christ has done. What Christ has done will never change and how God the Father feels about Christ will never change. Therefore, our new identity can never change. This is one of the most important and most freeing truths we can ever come to understand and enjoy – it's the truth that has changed my life and the lives of countless others.

The security of Christian identity is powerfully expressed in the popular worship song *Who You Say I Am*. The song is a reflection on the wonder of Christian identity and illustrates the confidence that followers of Jesus can have in our identity because we know that it is based purely on what God says of us with that rooted in what Christ has done:

> I am chosen, not forsaken.
> I am who You say I am.
> You are for me, not against me.
> I am who You say I am.
>
> Who the Son sets free, is free indeed.
> I'm a child of God.
> Yes, I am.[3]

Christian identity allows us to confidently know and embrace who we are.

The transformation into Christian identity

All of this is nicely illustrated in Paul's famous summary of the gospel in Ephesians 2:1–10, a passage that is all about a transformation of identity.

Paul starts by talking about the bad identity that is true of all of us so long as we live in rebellion against God: we are sons of disobedience (Eph. 2:2), children of wrath (Eph. 2:3) and, ultimately, spiritually dead (Eph. 2:1). But then he speaks of the transformation in identity that comes to Christians: we are made alive (Eph. 2:5), saved from the wrath we deserve (Eph. 2:5), seated in heavenly places (Eph. 2:6) and become God's new creations (Eph. 2:10).

And how does this change of identity come about? All through the work of Christ. Christian identity is rooted firmly in what Christ has done. Paul includes two motifs that stress this point.

The first is the motif of being 'in Christ'. This is one of Paul's favourite concepts. It speaks of believers being united with or hidden in Christ such that what is true of him is also true of us. The concept always makes me think of morphsuits, those spandex outfits that cover the entirety of the wearer's body. When you look at someone in a morphsuit, you see them, but you can't see them without, at the same time, seeing the morphsuit. In a similar way, God looks at Christians and sees us, but he can't look at us without also seeing Christ.

It's through our union with Christ that we receive the blessings of salvation and the new identity that they bring. It is 'together with Christ' that we have been made alive (Eph. 2:5), 'in Christ' that we have been seated in heavenly places (Eph. 2:6), and it is 'in Christ Jesus' that we have been created by God as his workmanship (Eph. 2:10). We are new creations with a new identity because we have been united with Christ.

The second motif through which Paul stresses the fact that salvation and our new identity are based on the work of Christ is that of the grace of God. It is by this grace that we are saved (Eph. 2:5). Paul helps us to understand what grace is by describing it as God's kindness to those who are in Christ Jesus (Eph. 2:7). There is nothing special about those who are united to Christ. Outside of Christ, Christians are just as much sons of disobedience and children of wrath as every other person. And yet God is wonderfully kind to us, uniting us with his son, saving us, and giving us a new identity. This is grace: God's favour shown to those who are utterly undeserving. God's grace isn't like receiving a gift from your best mate; it's like receiving a gift from the friend or acquaintance whom you have most hurt, offended or perhaps just ignored. It is not a gift we should expect or deserve; it's a gift we would never expect and could never deserve.

And God can show us this grace because of what he has done through Christ. This is not a great miscarriage of justice; it's not God just choosing to overlook the sins of some. It's God enacting his glorious plan of salvation in which he makes a way that he can maintain his righteousness and yet he can declare unrighteous sinners to be righteous (as Paul explains in Rom. 3:21–26).

All of this is summed up by Paul in Ephesians 2:8–10. Salvation – through which we receive this new identity – is by grace. It's not something we do, whether by earning it through our performance (as in 'others decide') or discovering it within (as in 'I decide'). Rather, it's a gift: received, not achieved, not discovered or created by us (Eph. 2:8–9).

And it's on the basis of this new identity that we are now to live (Eph. 2:10). What we do is not irrelevant, but it flows out from, rather than into, who we are. We are now God's workmanship, his new creations in Christ, and with this new identity we are called into a new way of living. Previously we walked in the way of the world, living in trespasses and sins. Now we are to walk in the way prepared for us by God, living in the good works he has set out before us. Our new identity should affect how we live. As we'll see, this has big implications for us when we think about sexuality and gender.

Does this mean that all Christians are basically the same to God? What about our many differences – different likes, dislikes, personalities, passions, and gifts? Does God not see those? Does he not care about who we are as individuals? He does, and he delights in our diversity. Many of those things are part of how we have been fearfully and wonderfully made by God and how he has uniquely shaped and gifted us. But they're not designed to be the basis of our identity – our controlling self-understanding. Remember, there are lots of things that are true of us – including lots of good things – that are not part of our identity. They are how we are, not who we are.

I guess it's a bit like a father or a mother who has multiple children. A good parent will love all of their children just because they are their children. The children don't have to earn the parent's love; they are loved simply because they are their parent's child. But that doesn't mean the parent doesn't see and value the unique differences between their children. One might love sport, while another lives for music. One might be naturally gifted at helping people solve problems, while another might be great at making people feel loved and welcomed. The parents can love their children because they are their children and yet still recognize their individuality. The same is true of us and God.

Evaluating 'God decides'

'God decides' is the best way of finding who we are because, in human identity and Christian identity, it can provide us with healthy identities that have many strengths compared to those offered by 'others decide' and 'I decide'.

'God decides' is the best way of finding who we are because it *releases us from pressure*. In 'others decide', we have the pressure to perform, to continue living up to the criteria, so that we can maintain a healthy identity. This can easily lead to perfectionism, fear of failure, and becoming a workaholic. In 'I decide', we have the pressure either to discover who we are by working through the mess of our feelings and desires, or to create our own identity.

Since human identity and Christian identity are received, not achieved or discovered, they take the pressure off. Human identity is already true of all of us, and to receive Christian identity, all we have to do is to accept the gift that is being offered to us. It is not dependent on our performance but on Christ's performance. Forming our identity based on who God says we are has the potential to be wonderfully freeing truth if we receive and embrace what he says.

My preoccupation with what other people thought about me caused me to be a workaholic to an unhealthy level. Without being fully aware of it, I was striving to impress people and to win their approval through my work. It was exhausting and often left me exhausted. 'God decides' identity gives me a way out of that. I'd be lying if I said I don't sometimes slip back into some workaholic tendencies, but knowing that my identity, and with it my worth and value, are rooted in what God says about me, not in what I can achieve through my work, empowers me to get a better balance in life. I still want to work hard, and I still want to bless others through my work, but I haven't got to prove myself through my work, and so I can stop, I can slow down, and I can take proper rest time. The pressure is off.

This truth also offers us *freedom from insecurity*. In 'God decides', our identity is secure. Our identity as those who bear God's image is stable and unchanging because it is rooted in how God has created us. It is an identity that can never change and is therefore secure. And Christian identity is stable and unchanging because it is based on the work of Christ and what God the Father thinks about that work. The work of Christ is completed and is not going to change, and what God thinks about it is not going to change either. We receive this identity through our union with Christ, which is also something that cannot change. The security of a 'God decides' identity can free us from the insecurity that can plague us under 'others decide' because we know we might fail to meet the criteria by which people evaluate us, or under 'I decide' because we know that what we find inside might change or be unclear.

One of the reasons a 'God decides' identity can offer freedom from pressure and insecurity is that it is *supported by an authority*. Both 'others decide' and 'I decide' identities suffer from a lack of support from authority: if different people view and evaluate you differently in 'others decide', who gets to dictate who you really are? And if you find different, perhaps conflicting, feelings or desires inside yourself, or what some might consider to be bad desires, how do you choose which ones reveal who you really are? All of this adds pressure and creates insecurity. But in 'God decides', we receive our identity from one who has authority to dictate who we really are because he made us, and it makes sense that our identity should come from our Creator. It's an identity supported by the ultimate authority.

I'm grateful that I have an identity rooted in a clear authority. If I was left to fashion my identity on the basis of my feelings and desires, I wouldn't know who I was. I'd be feeling huge pressure and huge insecurity as I tried to find the identity that would lead me into my best life. Do I embrace my desire to have lots of money and lots of stuff or my desire to bless others with my time and my resources (often the two don't go together very well!)? Do I embrace my desire to move to a big city or my desire to stay committed to sharing life with my close friends in a small town? Do I follow my desire to eat a lot of Big Macs or my desire to have six-pack abs? Allowing God to tell me who I am and how to experience my best life frees me from the pressure and anxiety I'd feel if it was all on my shoulders.

Finally, Christian identity allows us to *engage healthily with feelings and desires*. In 'others decide', identity is formed through supressing our feelings and desires so that we can conform to the expectations of others and live up to the criteria. Feelings and desires are suppressed and ignored. In 'I decide', identity is formed by embracing our feelings and desires so that we can be authentic. Both supressing and indiscriminately embracing our feelings and desires is unhealthy. Christian identity allows us to acknowledge our feelings and desires and to respond to them and steward them in the ways that God has revealed will be the most life-giving for us.

There's much more that could be said. But these points alone show that 'God decides' is, by far, the best way of making identity.

I am who God says I am

'God decides' is the best way of answering the question 'How do I find who I am?' When God decides, all humans are given the foundation of creation in God's image and all are invited to receive the very best and most life-giving form of identity: Christian identity.

For me, embracing and experiencing Christian identity has been truly life changing. I now know that I am not the freak and weirdo I so easily assume other people think I am. And I am not my sexuality or any other feeling or desire I might find within. I am a new creation in Christ, one saved by the grace of God. I am fully known and fully loved. I am a child of God.

Questions for reflection and discussion

- Where do we see the 'God decides' approach to identity illustrated in Scripture?
- What makes the 'God decides' approach to identity so good? Which of these strengths excites you the most?
- Who does God say you are?
- How should the 'God decides' approach to identity affect the way we interact with and treat other people?

5

'God decides' identity, sexuality and gender

Christian identity – an identity given by God – is the best foundation from which to live out our sexuality and gender. This has been my experience. Christian identity allows me to acknowledge the reality of my attraction to guys, and it also allows me to acknowledge the reality that my personality and preferences often align more with what is traditionally deemed feminine than with what is deemed masculine. Christian identity allows me to acknowledge these realities while living free from shame, secure in the fact that the only one whose opinion really matters fully knows me and fully loves me. And this gives me a solid foundation from which to establish how best to live out my sexuality and gender in such a way that I can thrive and flourish.

'God decides' identity and the opinion of others

In 'God decides' identity, Christian identity frees us from the opinions of others. It is therefore the best antidote to shame.

As we've seen, shame is a problem that can arise when we allow others to decide who we are. If our sense of self is shaped by what others think of us, and if they think there is something shameful about us, we come to experience shame.

But in Christian identity, who we are is not influenced by how others evaluate us or what they think of us. People may judge us or think badly of us, but we know that there is only one opinion that really matters, and we know that his opinion of us is based on who we are in Christ.

The apostle Paul understood this. Aware that some in the Corinthian church were critical of him and questioned his effectiveness as an apostle, he tells them, 'As for me, it matters very little how I might be evaluated by you or by any human authority. I don't even trust my own judgment on this point. My conscience is clear, but that doesn't prove I'm right. It is the Lord himself who will examine me and decide' (1 Cor. 4:3–4 NLT).

The low view that some of the Corinthians had of Paul didn't bother him. He knew that the evaluations of others, or even his own evaluation of himself, were not what mattered. What really mattered was God's evaluation of him. God decided who he was and so what other people said was not important.

This reality can give us an incredible confidence. Think of the confidence expressed by Elsa in *Let It Go*. By the end of the song, her sense of self has developed to a point where she can shrug off the opinions of others with a defiant hair flick. As we've seen, her confidence was actually misplaced: what she finds inside is not a good basis for her identity. (For one thing, being true to herself has plunged the people of Arendelle into an eternal winter!) But Christian identity gives us a true basis for that sort of confidence. Listening to who God says we are means our sense of self can stand strong in the face of the attempts of others to question or undermine our worth and value.

'God decides' identity and LGBTQ+ shame

This is why Christian identity is the best answer to the shame that LGBTQ+ people can so easily experience.

Of course, we must actively work to see an end to the cause of LGBTQ+ shame – discrimination and stigma. It's actually human identity – that universal element of a 'God decides' identity – that necessitates this. We know that all people are created in the image of God and so are worthy of honour and respect. The image of God reminds us that every human life has great value and inherent dignity. It's because of this truth that we should be challenging the negative assessment of LGBTQ+ people that so often leads to experiences of shame.

But even more powerful than changing the opinion of others is changing the source of our identity. We can't always change the other players in the game, but we can remove ourselves from the game. Christian identity removes us from a position where our identity is shaped by the opinions of others and frees us from the impact that those opinions can have on us.

I still sometimes hear people make derogatory or prejudiced statements about gay people. I still sometimes hear things that imply I am not only different but somehow weird or lesser because I'm attracted to guys. But choosing to root my identity in what God says about me, allowing only him to dictate who I am, helps me to not let those words shape my view of myself. Knowing who God says I am gives me some armour with which I can protect myself from lies that might try to creep in through the opinions of other people.

In Christian identity, we are fully known and yet fully loved. And that can never change. Because of this, Christian identity provides true and lasting freedom from shame.

'God decides' identity, feelings and desires

In the best form of identity available to us, Christian identity, who we are is rooted in our relationship to God, not in what we feel to be true, what we desire, or who we choose to be. This means what we find inside doesn't reveal who we are. Therefore, we don't need to embrace what's inside to find ourselves or to enjoy our best life. Our feelings and desires describe us, but they don't define us.

On the basis of the solid foundation of Christian identity, we are free to acknowledge, assess and respond to our desires and feelings. And this is just what Scripture teaches us to do.

Scripture acknowledges that all of us experience a whole mixture of desires – some good, some bad, and some a mixture of both.[1] I'm sure we can all relate to this. Think back over your day so far and the desires you have experienced. Some will have been good desires that drew you to good things, some will have been bad, and they will have tried to draw you to bad things, some will have had the potential to do both. Experiencing this mixture of good and bad desires is an inevitable part of existence in this age, and it always will be.

It is our responsibility to assess these desires and respond to them well. Those that are good can be nourished and expressed in appropriate ways, but those that are bad are to be starved and resisted.[2] The New Testament is very clear about the responsibility we as Christians have to respond rightly to bad desires: we are to abstain from them (1 Peter 2:11), put them to death (Col. 3:5), and flee from them (1 Tim. 6:9–11). We do this through the power of the Holy Spirit (Gal. 5:16; Rom. 8:13). Our desires may not be under our control, but our response to them is. Martin Luther, the Protestant reformer, quotes an earlier Christian who summarized this nicely: 'Dear brother, you can't prevent the birds in the air from flying over your head, you can easily take care that they make no nest in your hair.'[3]

How do we establish which desires are good and which are bad? We measure them against the teaching of Scripture. We can't just trust our own sense of what is good and what is bad. And we can't trust the world around us (Rom. 12:2). We can only trust God.

When it comes to our feelings – our intuitive beliefs about the world – these too need to be measured against Scripture. Real truth can only exist because there is one who is the truth (John 14:6). We are not the ones who determine what is true. We can't just trust that our feelings about what is true are actually correct. We all know how easy it is to feel that something is true even when in reality it is not. We need to examine what we feel to be true so we can then be equipped to respond well to those feelings.

This understanding of identity, desires and feelings equips us to approach the realities of sexuality and gender.

'God decides' identity and sexuality

Sometimes things that seem to have a fairly basic surface meaning are actually hiding a much deeper, more significant meaning. Take the *Wizard of Oz*, as an example. On the surface, it is a nice story about a young girl going on an unlikely adventure. But many believe that hidden behind that surface-level meaning is a deeper meaning: a picture of American politics and economics in the late nineteenth century. Sometimes, things have a deeper meaning.

The Bible shows us that human sexuality is one of those things. When we turn to Scripture, we find that our sexual desires are deeply meaningful. On the surface they seem to be about one thing, but when Jesus comes, we see they're actually about so much more. We might think sexual desires are about pleasure or forming relationships that will produce children – and they are about those things. But there's a deeper meaning too. Ultimately, our sexual desires are meant to be about God!

Sexual desire is designed to illustrate to us God's passionate desire for us, and marriage relationships are designed to reflect the relationship between Christ and the Church. They are like an architectural model, giving a foretaste – even if a limited one – of something greater and something to come. This is why, throughout Scripture, God speaks of his relationship with his people in terms of sex and marriage. When people turn away from God to worship idols, it is described in terms of prostitution or adultery,[4] while God's love for and relationship with his people is often spoken of using the imagery of sexuality and marriage.[5] We might think the language of sex and marriage is a bit intense for God to use of his relationship with us – but that's the point. God really is that passionate about us and that committed to us.

Our sexual desires are designed to help us understand God's longing for us to be in relationship with him, the deep love he has for us, and the great offence of our sin against him. In this way, sexuality is meant to point beyond itself to deeper, more fundamental desires and to a bigger and more meaningful story. Our sexual desires are not designed to completely fulfil us; rather, they are meant to point us to the one relationship that truly can.[6]

Understanding this helps us respond well to our sexuality, because understanding why something exists helps us know how to use it. If I come across a tool or a kitchen implement that I've never seen before, I might try to apply it to various uses, but chances are that if I don't know what it's actually for, I won't be able to use it very effectively, and I may actually end up doing some damage with it. The same is true with our sexualities. If we don't know what our sexual desires are really about, we run the risk of responding to them badly, or even in ways that do damage.

Putting it into practice

Understanding what sexual desires are about helps us know how to respond to them and makes sense of the Bible's parameters for sex. The Bible presents two options for how we steward our sexual desires: heterosexual marriage or celibate singleness.

Heterosexual marriage is the only context in which sexual activity is acceptable to God because it is the only context in which acting on our sexual desires can reflect the bigger story they are designed to tell. If sex is about Christ and the Church, then sex can only be rightly enjoyed in a relationship of covenant commitment – a marriage – reflecting the covenant commitment of Christ to the Church. This relationship must be between two, because Christ and the Church are two, and it must be between two who are different, because Christ and the Church are different.

The other way we can steward our sexuality is in celibate singleness. This might sound odd – how can we steward sexual desires into not having sex? They can be stewarded this way because we know that sexual desires are actually about more than sex. The sexuality of those who are single isn't wasted: our desires can still teach us about God. And not indulging and acting on those desires now is a way of living out the reality that sexuality is not the route to fulfilment but points us to the relationship that is. Stewarding our sexuality into celibate singleness while enjoying the greater relationship to which sexual desire is meant to point us is a way of acknowledging the deeply meaningful nature of sexual desire.

This means that the Bible's teaching on sex is really good news for single people like me. As a single, celibate guy, my singleness reminds me that Jesus can fulfil me in a way that no human relationship could. When I feel the force of sexual desire, it reminds me of the force of God's passionate love for me. And when I look in on healthy marriages, I get an insight into God's unwavering commitment to me and a reminder of his self-sacrificial love for me.

In God's plan, single people are not missing out on something that's necessary for human fulfilment. We still get to enjoy the relationship that truly is necessary for fulfilment. And the Bible's teaching releases us from the pressure that we can so often feel from our culture to be having sex. It's good news for those who don't feel they can enter into an opposite-sex marriage, good news for those who don't feel they want to marry, and even good news for those who might long to be married but for whom that wish never becomes a reality.

Christian identity also allows us to acknowledge that all of our sexualities are affected by sin. Every part of God's good creation has been touched by the effects of our corporate rebellion against God. Sexuality is no exception to that.

This is something we all know. Some will have experienced the impact of sin on sexuality through things that have been done to us. We may feel acutely aware of the reality that sexuality has been affected by sin, and we may find that the sin-affected sexuality of others has shaped our view of who we are. For those who have had such experiences, Christian identity can be part of how God helps us to find hope and healing.

Turning to think of our own sexual desires, we will all be aware that these are not always good. God has given us a sexuality so that from it we can learn about him as we steward it into opposite-sex marriage or celibate singleness. And yet, so often we allow our sexual desires to become about us, not about God. Rather than receiving sexual desires as an opportunity to learn about God, we receive them as an opportunity to have some fun. Rather than seeing them as a way we can give ourselves to another who is different from us and to whom we have committed, mirroring Christ's giving of and commitment of himself to us, we see them as a way to get what we want from another.

Our sexuality is a good gift given to us by God. But like all the good gifts God has given us in creation, sexuality has been damaged and distorted by sin. This is true for each one of us.

Christian identity allows us to acknowledge this reality. It allows us to seek, with the Spirit's help, the ability to acknowledge the good in our desires, but to give no foothold for the bad – to be blessed by the purposes for which God has given us a sexuality, but to flee from the ways the enemy would seek to use it for our harm. It allows us, with the Spirit's help, to express our sexuality in line with God's purposes for it, in marriage or singleness. And it allows us to do all this while knowing that we are perfectly and unendingly loved, even on the days when we struggle to steward our sexuality rightly.

As a guy who is same-sex attracted, Christian identity allows me to acknowledge the reality of my sexuality and not feel the need to hide it or feel ashamed about it. From this foundation it allows me to understand my sexual desires through the teaching of Scripture and then to choose to steward them in line with what God has revealed in his word. In doing this, I'm not denying who I am; I am living out my best identity as a human, and therefore sexual, being, but most importantly as a child of God.

'God decides' identity and gender

Many of us at different times in our life and to different extents may have questions about our sex and gender. We may have the occasional fleeting thought that in certain ways we're not really like other men or women. We may live with a constant lingering sense that we don't really make the cut as a real man or a real woman or that the very concept of being a man or a woman doesn't fit for us. For others, the experience can be more sustained and pronounced: a sense that we have been totally misunderstood. Perhaps it's that people think we're a man, but we feel we're a woman. This experience might be accompanied by significant and upsetting discomfort with the form of our body and the way others view and interact with us. People with this sort of experience might identify as transgender.

What does the Bible's teaching on identity have to say to us in the midst of these experiences?

First, human identity reminds us that no matter what our experience of gender we are made in the image of God. Being made in the image of God means that we have value and dignity, and we are deserving of honour and respect.

This truth should shape both the way we view ourselves and the way we view others. Sadly, many people, including Christians, have often not remembered this fundamental truth. Too often we have not shown to those who are questioning their gender or who identify as transgender the love, honour and respect of which all people are deserving. The reality of human identity should challenge the heart attitude with which we approach this topic and, more importantly, the people affected by it.

But the Bible helps us to go further. Scripture shows that God relates to us as men and women, not based on how we feel or what others think of us but based on how he has created us. This should be unsurprising to us once we have understood how the best form of identity – 'God decides' identity – works: who we are flows from our position in relation to the God who made us and what he declares to be true of us based on that relationship. This includes our relationship as creatures of the Creator.

One of the very first things we are told about humans in Scripture is that we are created in two types: male and female (Gen. 1:27). And in Genesis 1, our creation as male and female is placed in parallel with our creation in God's image. That's really important.

The image of God is an identity that is given to us by God. It is dependent purely on how he relates to us and what he says about us. The same is true for our identity as male or female, as a man or a woman. It doesn't depend on how we feel, but on how God relates to us and what he says about us.

And the way that God speaks to us about this part of who we are is through our bodies. In a biblical worldview, the body is not a container for our true self, as it often is for those who follow an 'I decide' approach to identity. Rather, the body is a core part of us. We don't *have* a body. We *are* a body.[7]

And Genesis 1 shows us that our identity as a man or woman is linked to the body God has given us. Immediately after it's stated that God creates us as male and female, we are given the commission to be fruitful, multiply and fill the earth (Gen. 1:28). Fulfilling this command requires the union of two people who have different bodies, a male and a female. This combination of humanity's creation as male and female and the commission to procreate affirm what modern science also recognizes: our body's orientation towards reproduction is what determines whether we are a man or a woman.[8] God tells us who we are – whether a man or a woman – through our bodies.[9]

Putting it into practice

Living out our God-given identity will always be best for us, and so this explains why the Bible expects males to live as men and females to live as women. But what does this mean? Well, that's actually a point on which the Bible doesn't have a lot to say. There are a few commands that are sex-specific (e.g. Eph. 5:22–28), but these seem to be restricted to specific roles that men and women play in a marriage or church context, and Christians hold a variety of views about these roles, both on whether they are present in Scripture and whether they are still relevant today. The Bible also seems to teach that our external presentation – how we dress, how we style our hair etc. – should demonstrate to others our identity as a man or a woman, in line with the conventions of our culture (e.g. Deut. 22:5; 1 Cor. 11:2–16). This also means we shouldn't seek to present as if we were of a gender that is different to our biological sex. Beyond this, the Bible gives us a lot of freedom in how we express being a man or a woman.[10]

This is all really important for people who identify as transgender or who experience gender dysphoria. The Bible's teaching on identity shows us that who we are as a man or a woman is not dictated by what we feel inside, but by who God says we are through how he has created us. This means that for those whose internal sense of gender clashes with their biological sex, transitioning is not the best or the right response.[11] God calls all of us to live out the identity he has given us through our bodies.

But this doesn't mean that transgender people have to start conforming to the restrictive gender stereotypes of our culture. That is not what God asks of us. As we've said, the Bible gives us a lot of freedom in how we live as a man or a woman, calling us only to certain roles in the context of marriage and church and to express our biological sex in how we present to others. This means that where restrictive stereotypes are a contributing factor to the distress of gender dysphoria, transgender people can find release from the cultural pressure to conform in those ways.[12]

This reality is borne out in the stories of detransitioners – those who previously identified as transgender and had transitioned to live as the opposite sex but have subsequently reverted to living in line with their biological sex. In such stories, it is sometimes noted that a better understanding of gender stereotypes and of the body's role in defining who we are as a man or a woman could have helped facilitate a better handling of experiences around gender. One detransitioner reflects, 'I would have liked it if more role models were around showing me women don't have to fit rigid stereotypes.' Another has said that a better understanding of these things 'would have allowed me to understand that being a woman is not fitting into stereotypes'.[13] There's something freeing about our identity as a man or a woman being rooted in the body God has given us.

And this truth is also really important for those of us who might not experience gender dysphoria or identify as trans but who feel a level of discomfort with our gender.

Many people live, often secretly, with a niggling sense of not really making the cut as a real man or a real woman. We look at others and think that they are a good example of what it should mean to be a man or a woman, but we look at ourselves and feel we just don't measure up. This can cause us to try to fit in by putting on a persona, or it can cause us to withdraw from those we deem real men or women because we find them intimidating.

This was my story. Although my sense of being a girl trapped in a boy's body faded away as I entered my teenage years, I continued to feel that I didn't really make the cut as a real man. I'd look at the guys around me and the guys in popular media and they were clearly proper men – they liked the right things, were good at the right things, and found it easy to get along with other men. I, on the other hand, barely ever liked the same things as most other guys, I was rubbish at the things that guys seemed to be good at, and I was too intimidated by other men to get along well with them. I would always hang out with the girls, rather than the guys. And to be honest, I still secretly held the wish that I could be one of the girls. I wasn't too fussed about having a different body, but if the guys and girls were doing separate things, I would always hope I'd get to go with the girls.

But recognizing the truth that my identity as a man is given to me by God and is stable and static was truly life changing. I still remember the moment when I realized that Genesis 1:27 meant I was a man no matter how I felt, how well or badly I seemed to fit in, or what other people thought about me. I realized I am a man because God says I'm a man, and no one and nothing can change or challenge that.

I realized that all the things about me that I thought were different – my personality, likes and dislikes – didn't change the fact I was a man. I could be a man – a real man – and still be me. I realized that knowing *who* I am gives me the freedom to be *how* I am.

As I've shared my journey with others, I've found that lots of people say they can relate. It seems that many of us feel that we don't really qualify as a real man or a real woman. The misuse of gender stereotypes that is so prominent in our culture and often also in our churches has robbed us of the freedom God wants us to enjoy by knowing who he says we are.[14] I think lots of us could benefit from knowing who we are so we can enjoy how we are.

Embracing our best identity

Many people look at my life and think that God has asked me to deny who I really am. Others think I have been so affected by LGBTQ+ shame that I have become a victim of internalized homophobia and need help to be able to accept my true self.

But as a follower of Jesus, I know that neither my sexuality nor my gender is my identity – I am not what I feel or what I desire. And I know that I have incredible value and worth because I am made in the image of God and am loved by God the Father with the same love with which he loves God the Son. I know that I am a child of God, and my best life is found by living out the pattern that my father in heaven has given me in his word. God doesn't ask me to suffer by denying who I am: he has invited me to thrive by embracing who he says I am.

Questions for reflection and discussion

- How does 'God decides' identity equip us to battle against shame?
- How does the 'God decides' approach to identity equip us to handle our experiences of sexuality?
- How does recognizing the deep meaningfulness of sexuality impact the way you think and feel about your experience of sexuality and how you will seek to steward your sexuality in the future?
- How does the 'God decides' approach to identity equip us to handle our experiences of gender?
- When we know *who* we are, we are free to be *how* we are. What does this look like for you?

6

Experiencing your best identity

When I realized that I had been allowing others to decide who I was and that I was living with a totally wrong and destructive identity, I was kind of shocked. I was shocked because I knew the content of Christian identity. I had been reading and studying the Bible for years. I had heard brilliant teaching on Christian identity. I had even done a fair bit of teaching on the topic myself. (In fact, I'd even written a book on the subject!)[1] How could I be living with such an unhealthy identity? Because it's easy to *know* who God says we are but not to *experience* who he says we are. Experiencing who God says we are requires some action.

Here are a few quick tips on how we can be proactive in experiencing 'God decides' identity.

Know yourself

We can miss out on experiencing the goodness of Christian identity because we are actually allowing either others or ourselves to decide who we are. This can happen so easily because these ways of making identity are part of the water we swim in. And in the same way that a fish doesn't notice water, we can easily not notice that we are looking for our identity in the wrong place. The water we're swimming in may be from our own past – perhaps we are so used to finding our identity in a certain way that it's second nature to us and we do it without even realizing. Or the water can be the culture we live in, where identities based on 'others decide' and 'I decide' are the norm.

If we want to enjoy Christian identity, we need to become alert to where we are most susceptible to finding our identity outside of what God says about us. We need to become aware of the water in which we're swimming. I know that I am most susceptible to finding my identity in what other people think about me. I've come to recognize that most of the times when I feel stressed, angry or low are because of my preoccupation with the opinions of others. Most of my weaknesses are rooted in the same thing – it's the reason I can often be a perfectionist and a workaholic. Knowing this helps me to spot times when I'm allowing others to dictate who I am and equips me to be proactive about allowing what God says to shape how I view myself.

Have a think about which way of finding identity you are most susceptible to. Are you more likely to be shaped by what people think about you or by what you find inside? It may be that both are a battle for you. Now try and dig a little deeper: Whose opinions are you particularly affected by? What part of what's inside you do you most easily value as the real you? Why is this the way of finding identity that you are most naturally drawn to?

It's also helpful to know what wrong beliefs about ourselves we are most susceptible to believing. Again, these can be rooted in our past and the things we, at one point, really believed to be true. For example, I know that I am still susceptible to the belief that I am a freak and a weirdo. If I'm in a context where I feel I don't really fit in or if someone makes a careless, throwaway comment about me, I can easily start to believe that lie about myself again. The wrong beliefs to which we're susceptible can also be rooted in the culture in which we live. The idea that I am my sexuality and that I will find my best life by embracing and acting on my sexual desires is so strong in my culture that I know I have to be aware of that as a wrong identity I could easily be tempted to adopt.

What wrong beliefs about yourself are you most susceptible to? Are there things you've believed strongly in the past (or are believing now)? Are there things culture would tell you about who you are that you know are a particular risk point for you? You might find it helpful to talk through these questions with a trusted Christian friend.

Know the truth

You can't live out your God-given identity if you don't know what it is. If knowing ourselves is about learning where we're susceptible to getting identity wrong, knowing the truth is about learning who God says we are.

The primary way we learn who God says we are is through the Bible. If we want to enjoy all that God has for us in Christian identity, there really is no substitute for regularly reading the Bible. And this isn't just about information: it's also about transformation. The Bible isn't just another book, it's the very words of God, and through those words God, by his Spirit, changes and transforms our understanding of who we are.

We can also be deliberate in learning the truth that we most need to grasp. It's always good to take a scattergun approach to knowing the truth of our identity: it never hurts to learn and to keep being reminded of all the many facets of who God says we are. But it can also be helpful to take a targeted approach. Making use of what we've learnt from coming to know ourselves better, we can find the elements of what God says that are the antidote to the lies we are particularly susceptible to believing. I have needed to be deliberate about targeting the lies I easily believe about myself – that I'm a freak and weirdo or that I'm not liked – with the truth of what God says, namely that I'm fearfully and wonderfully made, and that God delights over me with singing. Knowing yourself and knowing the truth allows you to be deliberate about rejecting wrongly formed identities and embracing your best identity.

Know how to experience the truth

But knowing the truth isn't enough. We also need to experience it in our hearts. How do we help the truth to make the short, but often difficult, journey from our heads to our hearts?

The answer will not be surprising to anyone who has been a Christian for more than a few weeks. The key things we can do are the normal practices of Christian life and worship. And that's exactly what we should expect. There's a reason that these practices have always been at the heart of Christian life – they help us to experience what God has done for us in Christ and the identity we receive from him. Each of these very normal Christian practices can play a key role in helping us to experience our identity.

Top of the list is *active participation in a local church*. Christian life is never meant to be lived alone. We grow and enjoy life with Jesus in community with his people. Our participation in a local church should help us to grow in experiencing our God-given identity.

Part of this will be through our engagement in corporate worship. When we gather to worship God together, we are gathering to glorify him. But, in his goodness, he has also ordained that worshipping together should build us up (1 Cor. 14:26). Our worship practices should be transformational, not just informational, and a growing experience of our identity should be a key part of the transformational impact of our corporate worship.

Another way that participation in a local church helps us to grow in Christian identity is through our relationships with each other. We get to be those who remind each other of who God says we are. We do this explicitly, speaking the truth to each other and challenging unhealthy identities. But we also do it implicitly through the way we interact. We get to demonstrate to each other that our worth and value are rooted in what God says of us, not how we feel or how well or badly we do something. We get to demonstrate that God loves us even when we make a mess of things by extending that same kind of love to each other. Through Christian friendship we grow in our identity, but we also get to help others grow.

We've already noted that the Bible is key to knowing the truth, but it also has an important role to play in experiencing the truth. Particularly powerful here is *meditating on Scripture*. To meditate on Scripture is to keep it in our mind, to chew over it and explore all its details, to allow it to work deeply into us. Meditating is different from just reading. Reading is like walking through a park to get to somewhere on the other side. You get a bit of a feel for what's going on and you might pick up on some of the sights, sounds and smells. But really, you're only getting a taste of what the park could offer you. Meditating is more like taking a long, slow, deliberate stroll through the park. You take your time, exploring different areas, taking in all that your senses can pick up. You leave knowing the park much better and with it having made a much greater impact on you. In the same way that we might need to slow down to fully enjoy a park, we often need to slow down to allow the truth of Scripture to work deeply into us.

Another key is *praying our identity*. There are lots of ways in which our identity can feature in our prayers. Christian identity is the basis on which we can confidently approach God in prayer. Jesus modelled this when he taught us to start our prayers, 'Our Father in heaven' (Matt. 6:9). Thanking God for our identity and reflecting on why it is so good helps us to experience it more powerfully.

We can also pray that God, by his Spirit, will help us to better experience our identity. One of the Spirit's roles is to reveal truth to us, and we can ask and invite him to do that for us. We can also pray this for other people. If you're ever not sure what to pray for a Christian friend, pray that they would more deeply know who they are in Christ. And if you get to actually pray with them, that's even better – while you're praying, you're asking God to do what he loves to do, you're reminding your friend of the importance of their identity in Christ, and you're reminding yourself!

Prayer and Scripture can also be combined. When we read in Scripture truths about who we are as Christians, we have an opportunity to pray that we would experience that truth and to pray it for others too.

A powerful way of moving truth from our head to our heart is to *sing the truth*. God has designed us in such a way that singing is a powerful thing. When we sing, we connect more deeply with what we're saying. That's why songs are used to express deep emotion. It doesn't matter how well or badly we can sing, what matters is that we're doing it. Singing the truth reminds us (and those around us) of who God says we are and pushes that truth deeper into our hearts.

An action plan

At this point you could just close this book, stick it on a shelf and think, 'Well that was an interesting read.' But doing that would be like unwrapping the best gift imaginable and then just ignoring it. Or it would be like learning you've inherited a great fortune and doing nothing with it. To make the time you've spent reading worthwhile, you've got to put this into action.

Hopefully this chapter has given you some ideas of how you can do that. Why not pause right now to think about and decide upon what you're going to do to help you to experience your best identity?

If you need a bit more help, here's an action plan you could use. Don't rush this. Journeying to experience our best identity is a marathon, not a sprint.

Step one – Know yourself

Take some time to reflect on these questions. Ask the Holy Spirit to bring things to mind and to help you answer the questions accurately. You might also find it helpful to discuss them with a close friend.

- Which approach to finding your identity comes most naturally to you?
- What specific wrong beliefs about yourself are you most susceptible to?
- What are the symptoms of these wrong beliefs, the impact they are having on your life?

Step two – Know the truth

Based on what you've identified about yourself, think about the truth that you need to know.

- What does the Bible say in response to the wrong ideas you are susceptible to believing about yourself?

If you're not sure what the Bible says, you might find it helpful to ask a Christian friend or a church leader.

Step three – Know how to experience the truth

Now you want to take some actions to help you start to believe the truth of who God says you are. This is all about helping what God says move down into your heart. Here are a few ideas of how you can do that:

- Immerse yourself in what God says – Take the Bible verses you identified in the previous step and find ways to immerse yourself in them. Stick them on Post-it Notes and place them in locations where you'll see them regularly or compile them on a single sheet that you can keep in your pocket, at your desk, or on your coffee table. Take moments throughout the day to focus on one of the verses. Read it, chew it over, pray it. Or at the start of each day choose a verse to live with that day – coming back to it, thinking about it, praying it as you go about your day.

- Battle using the truth – When you notice yourself being drawn back to a wrong idea about who you are, use the biblical truths you have identified to battle against that idea, replacing it with what God says. When you notice the symptoms of living with a wrong identity, pause to think what it is you're believing at that moment, and remind yourself instead of the truth of who God says you are.

- Create a playlist of songs – Find some Christian songs that will help you to focus in on who God says you are. Listen to these songs and meditate on the truths they contain. Sing these songs to declare to yourself your best identity. Pray these songs to ask that the truth they contain would make its way into your heart.

- Talk with friends – Tell close Christian friends what you've learnt about yourself and about who God says you are. Ask them to pray for you. Ask them to check in with you to see how you're doing at growing in experiencing your best identity. Ask them to remind you of who God says you are.

You'll be able to add your own ideas here. These examples are just a starting point.

Experiencing your best identity isn't something that happens without some effort, but all the effort will be worth it when you come to know, to experience and to enjoy who God says you really are. Your best identity is waiting for you. The question is, are you going to take hold of it?

Notes

Chapter 2: 'Others decide'

1 Alexis Petridis, 'Madonna: "I wanted to be somebody because I felt like a nobody"', *The Guardian* (https://www.theguardian.com/music/2019/jun/14/madonna-i-wanted-to-be-somebody-because-i-felt-like-a-nobody) (accessed 11 January 2021).

2 A fascinating book that makes this case is Matthew Todd, *Straight Jacket: How to be Gay and Happy* (Bantam Press, 2016). For a review of the research on LGBT mental health, see Andrew Bunt, 'LGBT and Mental Health: What's the Link?', *Living Out* (https://www.livingout.org/resources/articles/95/lgbt-and-mental-health-whats-the-link).

3 Will Young in Matthew Todd, *Pride: The Story of the LGBTQ Equality Movement* (André Deutsch, 2019), p.180.

4 'LGBT bullying more common than racist bullying in schools – poll', *Sky News* (https://news.sky.com/story/lgbt-bullying-more-common-than-racist-bullying-in-schools-11756325) (accessed 10 January 2021). The survey found homophobic bullying to be slightly more common than racist bullying, and considerably more common that bullying in relation to sex or religion.

5 'LGBT in Britain – Work Report', *Stonewall*, 2018 (https://www.stonewall.org.uk/system/files/lgbt_in_britain_work_report.pdf), p.7 (accessed 10 January 2021).

6 'LGBT in Britain – University Report', *Stonewall*, 2018 (https://www.stonewall.org.uk/system/files/lgbt_in_britain _universities_report.pdf), p.5 (accessed 10 January 2021).

7 'LGBT in Britain – Work Report', p.9.

8 'LGBT in Britain – University Report', p.7.

Chapter 3: 'I decide'

1 The following examples are taken from a talk by Tim Keller titled 'Culture and Identity', available at https://www .livingout.org/resources/articles/57/identity-in-christ -conference-culture-and-identity

2 'How To Find Yourself: 11 Ways To Discover Your True Identity', *A Conscious Rethink* (https://www.aconsciousrethink .com/10395/how-to-find-yourself/) (accessed 20 August 2021).

3 Some might see this as an unfair example: a desire to kill lots of people harms others, and so that's a clear reason to reject it as identity. But what if the person found some willing victims who wanted to be killed? If it was all between consenting adults, would we then say the person could embrace and express their self-declared identity? I expect most of us wouldn't. We all find it hard to apply this approach consistently and that suggests it's not a good way to find our identity.

4 Jeremy E. Sherman, 'Just Be True To Yourself? Not Quite?', *Psychology Today* (https://www.psychologytoday.com/gb /blog/ambigamy/201802/just-be-true-yourself-not-quite) (accessed 8 February 2021).

5 'Philip Schofield Opens up About Being Gay | This Morning', *YouTube* (https://www.youtube.com /watch?v=GNIbb-52lGU) (accessed 22 February 2021).

6 @davidwalliams on Twitter, 7 February 2020. Emphasis added. (https://twitter.com/davidwalliams/status /1225726939668918272) (accessed 22 February 2021).

7 @NicolaS09328429 on Twitter, 7 February 2020. Emphasis added. (https://twitter.com/NicolaS09328429/status /1225863691347865602) (accessed 22 February 2021).

8 @leta_edde on Twitter, 7 February 2020. Emphasis added. (https://twitter.com/leta_edde/status/1225847397407789056) (accessed 22 February 2021).

9 @memesoph4 on Twitter, 7 February 2020. Emphasis added. (https://twitter.com/memesoph4/status /1225821602484543489) (accessed 22 February 2021).

10 Quoted in Hannah Orenstein, 'Sam Smith's Instagram Caption About Using They/Them Pronouns Is So Powerful', *Elite Daily*. Emphasis added. (https://www.elitedaily.com/p /sam-smiths-instagram-caption-about-using-theythem -pronouns-is-so-powerful-18753636) (accessed 21 February 2021).

11 'Every Name's a Story #whatsyourname', *Starbucks Stories & News EMEA*. Emphasis added. (https://stories.starbucks.com /emea/stories/2020/whatsyourname) (accessed 21 February 2021).

12 See, for example, Lisa M. Diamond, 'Sexual Fluidity in Male and Females', *Current Sexual Health Reports* 8 (2016), 249–256, and 'Lisa Dimond on sexual fluidity of men and women', *YouTube* (https://www.youtube.com/watch?v =m2rTHDOuUBw) (accessed 8 February 2021).

13 Adrienne Matei, '"It's how I feel. It's not how you feel": four teens explain why they reject the gender binary', *The Guardian* (https://www.theguardian.com/lifeandstyle/2020

/jun/29/non-binary-four-teens-explain-gender-genderqueer-generation) (accessed 21 February 2021).

14 Primary among these would be sexual desire towards children. It is debated whether paedophilia should be considered a sexual orientation. The experience has many similarities with other orientations: 'Pedophilia, a sexual preference for prepubescent children, appears early in life, is stable over time, and directs the person's sexuality with regard to thoughts, fantasies, urges, arousal, and behaviour' (Michael C. Seto, 'Pedophilia' in Brian L. Cutler (ed.), *Encyclopedia of Psychology & Law* (SAGE Publications, 2008), 547–551 (p.547)). Some scholars therefore argue that paedophilia is a sexual orientation (e.g. Michael C. Seto, 'Is Pedophilia a Sexual Orientation?', *Archives of Sexual Behavior* 41 (2012), 231–236; Fred S. Berlin, 'Pedophilia and DSM-5: The Importance of Clearly Defining the Nature of Pedophilic Disorder', *The Journal of the American Academy of Psychiatry and the Law* 42 (2014), 404–407), while others oppose this idea (e.g. J. Paul Fedoroff, 'The Pedophilia and Orientation Debate and Its Implications for Forensic Psychiatry', *The Journal of the American Academy of Psychiatry and Law* 48 (2020), 146–150). In many ways, it depends on the working definition of 'sexual orientation'.

15 On trans-speciesism: Eliza Graves-Browne, 'What It Means to be Trans Species', *Vice* (https://www.vice.com/en/article/yvwknv/what-does-it-mean-to-be-trans-species); 'Why be human when you can be otherkin?', *University of Cambridge Research* (https://www.cam.ac.uk/research/features/why-be-human-when-you-can-be-otherkin). On

transableism, Sarah Boesveld, 'Becoming disabled by
choice, not chance: 'Transabled' people feel like impostors
in their fully working bodies', *National Post* (https://
nationalpost.com/news/canada/becoming-disabled-by
-choice-not-chance-transabled-people-feel-like-impostors
-in-their-fully-working-bodies), and Ashley P. Taylor, 'The
Complicated Issue of Transableism', *JSTOR Daily* (https://
daily.jstor.org/the-complicated-issue-of-transableism).

Chapter 4: 'God decides'

1 For example, as God prepares to rescue his people from
Egypt, he declares 'Israel is my firstborn son' (Exod. 4:22).
And when they have escaped from their slavery and come
to mount Sinai, God tells them that the covenant he is now
making with them will give them the opportunity to be his
'treasured possession among all peoples' as well as 'a
kingdom of priests and a holy nation' (Exod. 19:5–6). Who
they truly are flows from their relationship with God. In
the New Testament, both Jesus and the Apostles root the
identity of Christians in relationship with God and what he
says: Christians are Jesus' 'friends' (John 15:14), each being
a saint (Rom. 1:7), a temple of the Holy Spirit (1 Cor. 6:19),
part of a holy priesthood (1 Peter 2:5) and, supremely, a
child of God (1 John 3:1; also Rom. 8:14–16; 1 Peter 1:14).

2 This is a contested point. It's often claimed that the image is
damaged or even lost because of sin. This view rests
primarily on New Testament texts that seem to describe
salvation in terms of a restoration of the image. If the image
needs restoring, it must have been damaged. However,
there are good reasons to think the image is unaffected by

sin: (1) Scripture never explicitly states that the image is
damaged by sin; (2) the few references to the image after
the Fall never imply that it has been damaged (Gen. 5:1;
9:6; 1 Cor. 11:7; James 3:9); (3) the New Testament texts
that speak of transformation into the image of Christ focus
on Christ as God, not on Christ as the perfect human; (4)
the idea of the image being damaged introduces problems
about the value of life in light of the use of the image in
Genesis 9 and James 3. For a defence of this position, see
John F. Kilner, 'Humanity in God's Image: Is the Image
Really Damaged?', *JETS* 53/3 (Sept. 2010), 601–617.

3 *Who You Say I Am* Words and Music by Ben Fielding &
Reuben Morgan © 2017 Hillsong Music Publishing
Australia (Admin. by Hillsong Music Publishing UK).

Chapter 5: 'God decides' identity, sexuality and gender

1 This is illustrated in the language Scripture uses. In both
the Hebrew of the Old Testament and the Greek of the New
Testament, the most common words for desire have a
neutral meaning, and the exact nuance of a good or bad
desire is indicated by the context. In Hebrew, the root is חמד
(*chāmad*) and can be used positively (e.g. Ps. 19:10; 68:16)
or negatively (e.g. Exod. 20:17; Prov. 12:12; Isa. 1:29). In
Greek, the verb ἐπιθυμέω (*epithumeō*) and noun ἐπιθυμία
(*epithumia*) can both be used positively (e.g. Luke 22:15;
Phil. 1:23; 1 Tim. 3:1) or negatively (e.g. Gal. 5:16–17; 1
Peter 2:11; 1 John 2:16).

2 At this point the question arises as to whether such bad
desires (often called concupiscence by theologians) are

themselves sin, in the sense of something for which an individual incurs guilt before God. The Catechism of the Catholic Church states that concupiscence is not sin (2515), describing it as only 'the tinder for sin' (1264). In contrast, Protestant theologians have tended to affirm the desires themselves as sin (e.g. John Calvin, *Institutes* 3.3.10; Herman Bavinck, *Reformed Dogmatics: Volume 3: Sin and Salvation in Christ* (Baker Academic, 2006), pp.142–144; Louis Berkhof, *Systematic Theology* (Banner of Truth, 1958), pp.233, 236). The question is not unimportant, but the answer doesn't much change the reality of the Bible's teaching on how to handle desires. That's what we'll focus on here.

3 Martin Luther, *Exposition of the Lord's Prayer* (James Nisbet & Co., 1844), p.89. I have modernized some of the more archaic elements of the translation in this quote.

4 For example, Deuteronomy 31:16; Judges 2:17; Psalm 106:39; Jeremiah 3:6–10; Ezekiel 16:15–43; Hosea 2:2–5; Revelation 17:1–2.

5 For example, Ezekiel 16:8–14; Hosea 2:14–20; 1 Corinthians 6:15–17; Ephesians 5:22–33; Revelation 19:7–9; 21:2, 9.

6 This is a point inspired by Sam Allberry, *7 Myths About Singleness* (Crossway, 2019), p.112.

7 We can see this, for example, in 1 Corinthians 6:12–20. Paul is responding to the fact that some of the Corinthians have been having sex with prostitutes. Those doing so may have defended their actions by arguing that bodies aren't important, but Paul's response shows the body to be a true and important part of who we are: the body is meant for

God, not immorality (1 Cor. 6:13). The body will one day be raised from the dead as Christ – embodied – was raised from the dead (1 Cor. 6:14). Our bodies are part of Christ's body (1 Cor. 6:15). We can sin against our bodies (1 Cor. 6:18). And our bodies are temples for God's Spirit (1 Cor. 6:19). The body is not of secondary importance; it is a core part of who we are.

8 Scientists recognize that the body's orientation towards reproduction is the only way of classifying males and females. For example, Lawrence S. Mayer & Paul R. McHugh, 'Sexuality and Gender: Findings from the Biological, Psychological, and Social Sciences', *The New Atlantis* 50 (2016), 10–143 (p.90): 'In biology, an organism is male or female if it is structured to perform one of the respective roles in reproduction. This definition does not require any arbitrary measurable or quantifiable physical characteristics or behaviors; it requires understanding the reproductive system and the reproduction process . . . There is no other widely accepted biological classification for the sexes.' Suggestions that the brain might determine sex (sometimes called 'Brain-Sex Theory') fail on the fact that there is no clear binary between male and female brains; there are only differences that are commonly, but not always, found in males and female brains.

9 This remains true even notwithstanding the reality of intersex conditions. In the rare cases where people with intersex conditions are not clearly either male or female, they are best understood as reflecting a combination of male and female rather than a third sex. See Preston Sprinkle, 'Intersex and Transgender Identities', *Living Out*

(https://www.livingout.org/resources/articles/84/intersex
-and-transgender-identities).

10 For more detail on the biblical basis for this position, see
Preston Sprinkle, *Embodied: Transgender Identities, the
Church and What the Bible Has to Say* (David C. Cook,
2021), pp.70–72, 90–94.

11 There is very little reliable research on the long-term
outcomes of transitioning. Most of the studies that do exist
consider only the first year or so after transition and exhibit
serious methodological limitations. A helpful summary
and evaluation of the available research can be found in
Preston Sprinkle, *Embodied: Transgender Identities, the
Church and What the Bible Has to Say* (David C. Cook,
2021), pp.188–192. Anecdotal evidence that transition may
not always be the best response to trans experience is found
in the growing number of detransitioners who are publicly
sharing their stories. See, for example *Post Trans*
(https://post-trans.com/) and *Detrans Voices* (https://www
.detransvoices.org/). See also, Lisa Marchiano, 'The Ranks
of Gender Detransitioners Are Growing. We Need to
Understand Why', *Quillette* (https://quillette.com/2020/01/02
/the-ranks-of-gender-detransitioners-are-growing-we
-need-to-understand-why). There are also calls for further
research into whether psychotherapeutic responses to
gender dysphoria may be more helpful than transitioning,
e.g., R D'Angelo et al., 'One Size Does Not Fit All: In
Support of Psychotherapy for Gender Dysphoria', *Arch Sex
Behav* (2020). Useful summaries of available research can
be found at statsforgender.org/medical-transition.

12 This is not all that should be said on a Christian response to transgender. It would be naïve to think that freedom from gender stereotypes will be enough to bring total peace to someone with severe gender dysphoria. For more on how Christians can give a rounded response to transgender experience which takes seriously the suffering of gender dysphoria, see Andrew Bunt, *People Not Pronouns: Reflections on Transgender Experience* (Grove Books, 2021).

13 Nele Peer Jongeling and Elie Vandenbussche, 'Gender Detransition: A Path Towards Self-Acceptance', pp.30–31 (https://post-trans.com/detransition-booklet).

14 For more on gender stereotypes, see Andrew Bunt, 'What Should We Do With Gender Stereotypes?', *Living Out* (https://www.livingout.org/resources/articles/52/what-should-we-do-with-gender-stereotypes).

Chapter 6: Experiencing your best identity

1 Andrew Bunt, *Who In Heaven's Name Do You Think You Are?: Exploring Your Identity in Christ* (Charis Books, 2015). As it happens, I think that book – which explores the content of Christian identity – is still useful. Hopefully the deeper understanding of how identity works provided here will provide a useful accompaniment to that earlier book.

Further reading

I've only been able to give a short introduction to identity, sexuality and gender in this small book. Here are some recommendations if you want to delve deeper into these topics.

On identity formation – the question 'How do I find who I am?'

Tim Keller, *The Freedom of Self-Forgetfulness: The Path to True Christian Joy* (10Publishing, 2015)

Chris Morphew, *Who Am I and Why Do I Matter?* (The Good Book Company, 2022)

Trevin Wax, *Rethink Yourself: The Power of Looking Up Before Looking In* (B&H Publishing, 2020)

Alan Noble, *You Are Not Your Own: Belonging to God in an Inhuman World* (IVP, 2021)

On the content of Christian identity – who God says you are

Andrew Bunt, *Who in Heaven's Name Do You Think You Are?: Exploring Your Identity in Christ* (Charis Books, 2015)

Paul Mallard, *An Identity to Die For: Know Who You Are* (IVP, 2020)

Terry Virgo, *God's Lavish Grace* (Monarch, 2004)

On sexuality and gender

Ed Shaw, *Purposeful Sexuality: A Short Christian Introduction* (IVP, 2021)

Preston Sprinkle, *People to Be Loved: Why Homosexuality Is Not Just An Issue* (Zondervan, 2015)

Ed Shaw, *The Plausibility Problem: The Church and Same-Sex Attraction* (IVP, 2015)

Andrew Bunt, *People Not Pronouns: Reflections on Transgender Experience* (Grove Books, 2021)

Preston Sprinkle, *Embodied: Transgender Identities, the Church and What the Bible Has to Say* (David C. Cook, 2021)

Carl R. Trueman, *Strange New World: How Thinkers and Activists Redefined Identity and Sparked the Sexual Revolution* (Crossway, 2022)

Acknowledgements

The seeds that have grown into this book were sown in some of my darkest days. In June 2018, I was in a very bad way. I was depressed and struggling to function, unaware at that that stage, that part of my problem was a failure to experience my best identity. At that point I was kindly granted some compassionate leave from my role at King's Church Hastings and Bexhill. I took the opportunity to go and stay with good friends in Winchester. The day after I arrived, my friend was going to a Living Out conference in London where Tim Keller would be speaking on identity in Christ. On paper, it probably wasn't a wise decision to go on a long day trip to London when I was meant to be resting and reflecting, but thankfully I couldn't resist. The teaching given by Tim Keller on that day sowed the seeds that in time came to help me out of the darkness in which I was living, and they grew and developed into this book. I am grateful to Tim Keller for what he brought at that event, gladly acknowledging how heavily influenced this book is by that day's teaching, and I am deeply grateful to God for orchestrating things to get me there.

In the months and years that have followed since, the seedlings that sprouted after that day have been lovingly nurtured by friends who refused to give up on me even when I was so often ready to give up on myself. As I came to realize and face fully the destructive and incredibly painful identity with which I was living, they listened to me, wept with me, held me, and helped me. I cannot sufficiently express my gratitude to them for their support. I'm genuinely not sure I would have made it through without them. Nat, Caner and Jo, Paul, Steve and Becky, Will and Paris – thank you.

In the time since I first wrote these words, Becky has gone to be with Jesus. The love, care and support that Becky showed me in our twelve years of friendship have been truly life changing for me. I will strive to live in the good of all that she taught me and inputted into me. It is with great gratitude to her and for her that I dedicate this book to her memory.

Another key ingredient which allowed the seeds sown on that day in London to grow and produce fruit was counselling. Nat, thank you for pushing and persisting until I agreed to give it a try. Mark, thank you for being such a gentle, patient, and caring counsellor, for helping me not to give up, but also not to avoid the pain I had to face. So much of this book is the result of our time together. I hope that in a small way it helps many others to experience something of the heart and the gift that God has given you.

As the growth from those seeds produced fruit in my own life, I began to have the privilege of sharing the good I was experiencing with others. I'm grateful for all the opportunities that I have had to speak on this topic and for the many people who have talked with me about it. As the book took shape, feedback from thoughtful and encouraging readers made it far better than it would otherwise have been. Thank you to Adam, Mike, Steve, Catherine, Ashleigh, Andy and Ed. A special thank you to Glynn whose perceptive comments helped me to iron out some weaknesses which I knew were present but which I hadn't quite managed to isolate or address. The weaknesses that remain are certainly my responsibility, but there are fewer of them thanks to all this helpful input.

Others also deserve a mention. Thanks to my editor Tom for his support with this project; the staff team and the whole church family at King's Church for your friendship and encouragement; Steve and Lori for providing me with such a lovely home environment in which to live, work and write; and the Living Out team for your friendship, encouragement, and support – it is so good not to be alone in the challenges of our unusual lives and area of ministry.

My biggest thank you goes to the one who has not only given me my best identity but has also intervened to make sure I get to experience it. What you say about me sounds too good to be true and yet it is. How wonderful that is.

May this book play a part in helping many others to come to experience this wonderful truth.

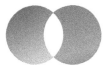

Living Out

We help people, churches
and society talk about
faith and sexuality.

livingout.org

CPSIA information can be obtained
at www.ICGtesting.com
Printed in the USA
JSHW080658051122
32626JS00005B/18